Ready, Set, Play!

Parents and Children Bonding Through Sports

Mark Schlereth and Mark Preisler

with Bryan Reardon

TRIUMPH
B O O K S

Library of Congress Cataloging-in-Publication Data
Ready, set, play! : parents and children bonding through sports /
    [Introduction by] Mark Schlereth and [preface by] Mark Preisler; with Bryan Reardon.
        p. cm.
    ISBN 978-1-60078-395-1
1. Sports for children—United States. 2. Sports for children—Social aspects—United States. 3. Children—Family relationships—United States. 4. Parent and child—United States. I. Reardon, Bryan.
    GV709.2.R43 2010
    796.083—dc22   2010023342

This book is available in quantity at special discounts for your group or organization. For further information, contact:

Triumph Books
542 South Dearborn Street
Suite 750
Chicago, Illinois 60605
(312) 939–3330
Fax (312) 663–3557
www.triumphbooks.com

Printed in U.S.A.
ISBN: 978-1-60078-395-1
Design by Sue Knopf

Contents

Preface | Mark Preisler

When I first sat down to write the preface for this book, my first thought was, *Who cares what I think?* My coauthor had a great NFL career and is a fabulous analyst at ESPN now. His kids are older than mine, and he's already proven himself to be a great father. On top of that, the contributors to this book are some of the most recognizable celebrities in this country. That's what you want to read about. Those are the stories everyone is interested in.

For weeks, I tried to figure out what I could add by sharing my own story. While I went about my normal routine, the question remained at the back of my mind. I would be at work at ESPN until the wee hours of the morning, helping fans across the country get the most up-to-date news and highlights from the nation's pastime on *Baseball Tonight*. Then I'd get home, pull out the computer, and try to come up with my own story. I had no idea it would be this hard, and I still wasn't convinced it was necessary.

Then early one Saturday morning, things became clear to me. It started like most Saturdays at the Preisler house. I got home from ESPN at about 3:00 AM. That night, like all nights, I had to stay at work until the final out of the final game—usually one on the West Coast.

I crept through the house. Everyone was asleep, and the last thing I wanted to do was wake them up. My body has gotten used to the schedule, but that doesn't mean I don't get exhausted. And that particular morning, I was exhausted.

Bed felt really good. When I hit the pillow, though, all the stresses and excitement of the day kept my eyes from closing right away. It wasn't me trying to come up with the idea for this preface, but just everyday life that kept me awake for another half an hour or so. Finally I managed to get to sleep. I'd say it was about 3:30 AM.

"Da-dee, where are you?"

It was a soft sound that woke me up. It came from down the hall. It's a sound that gets me out of bed almost every morning. My wife stirred, but she knew I was getting up. I glanced at the clock and it was 6:30 AM.

"Da-dee, where are you?"

The call came again, this time a little louder. I could hear my daughter's smile in the words. Her name is Francesca, but we call her Frankie. She's two and a half now but already in charge of the family. And she has this head of curly blond hair. It's her trademark, really.

So after three hours of sleep, I climbed out of bed. I think I groaned once. Who wouldn't? But as I walked down the hallway toward Frankie's room, I could hear her rustling around in her crib. It made me smile. It always does.

When I got to her room that morning, she was lying in her crib holding her precious Pooh Bear. Her bright eyes looked right into my heart. As usual, she asked for some orange juice. As usual, I said yes and trudged down to get it. After that, I picked her up and she gave me one of those hugs, wrapping herself around my neck and pulling as tightly as her little muscles could. It was enough to clear my mind from the fog of too little sleep.

Mark Preisler and daughter Frankie

"Daddy, sit on your knees," she said, so she could see me over the railing. "Do you have to go to work today?"

"Yes," I said. "But not 'til later."

"Can we go to the playground?" she asked.

"Sure," I said. "But later. I still have to go back to sleep."

We read for a while and played with her stuffed animals—Tigger, Pooh, Piglet—all the Disney characters. Who else? They *do* own ESPN, after all.

I was still a little tired, so I can't remember exactly what else we did. As this is our daily ritual, these mornings blend together in my mind sometimes. Regardless, we played for about an hour. Frankie looked up at me, and even at two and a half, she could see I was tired.

"Are you going back to sleep now, Daddy?" she asked.

"Yeah, honey," I answered.

Her little face crinkled up.

"You want to go running in a little while?" I asked.

Her smile came back then. "To the waterfall?"

"Definitely," I said, smiling back at her.

She walked me back to bed. I fell asleep right away because I knew I had to get up soon. I had a running date.

I woke up at 10:30. Frankie was standing next to the bed, staring at me.

"Are you awake?" she asked.

I smiled. "Yeah."

Her mom already had her dressed for the run. That means she had her little Nike headband on, the same kind I wear.

"You ready for our run?" I asked.

She did a little dance she does, and her blonde hair bounced around. "To the waterfall."

Frankie wanted to help me load the stroller into the car. I packed her some snacks—carrots and a muffin— and we headed out, waving good-bye to Mom. I live on a river, so it's a great place to run. Once I parked and got Frankie out of her car seat, she climbed into the jogger, and we headed out. Immediately she was directing the trip.

"Daddy, the water's that way," she told me.

I always listen, too. So I gave her the little bag of carrots and we were off. Frankie got quiet, enjoying her snack. The sun was out that morning, and although there was a chill in the air, it felt warm on my shoulders and face. Birds were singing all around me, and I felt this really profound peace. And my thoughts drifted to my own dad.

When I was just becoming an adult, I used to run with him a lot. It was our time to talk about things. I realize now that a lot of the things we talked about were part of my journey to becoming a man and eventually Frankie's father. Unfortunately, Dad passed away before she was born. It's my deepest disappointment.

My dad, Harvey Preisler, was a renowned cancer researcher and physician. But what I remember most about him is the four things he loved above all others. In order of importance: his family, science, the New York Football Giants, and the Brooklyn Dodgers. When the Dodgers left Brooklyn, however, the list dropped down to three things he loved most. Interestingly, when the Giants left Yankee Stadium and moved to the Meadowlands in New Jersey, it didn't faze him. He stayed a die-hard Giants fan for life.

While I was running that morning, glancing down to check on my daughter, I thought about the relationship I had with my dad. One of the things I remember most from my childhood is a science-experiment club that he signed me up for. I think I was about eight years old at the time. It was one of those clubs where a different experiment was mailed to the house each month. They were things like, "Build a baking soda volcano," and "See what happens to a copper penny when put in different liquids." I know that a lot of kids would be really into that kind of thing, but I wasn't.

At first, I felt awful. I knew what science meant to my dad. I was worried that if he thought I didn't like the experiments it would really disappoint him. But that's not what happened. He figured me out pretty quickly and, to my surprise, he ended my membership in the science club.

That was when he started concentrating more on taking me out back to throw the football. He knew how much I loved sports, and he supported that love. He knew, even though I was only eight, that the way to connect with me was through sports. He played with me. He took me to sporting events—by this time we were living in Buffalo, so it was Bills and Sabres games. He even coached my Little League team.

I'll never forget one day in Little League when I was pitching. I was having a bad day. I couldn't find the strike zone. My dad marched out to the mound in his dark socks and sandals and took me out of the game. I was crushed, but I learned two things. The first, something I wouldn't realize until my daughter was born, was that I wanted to be an active part of my kid's life—particularly through sports, which I believe is one of the best ways to make sure kids are active. The second was not to wear dark socks, or any socks for that matter, with sandals—particularly when being an active part of my kid's life.

When I was about nine or ten, my dad introduced me to running. We were already hitting a tennis ball around by then, too. I loved that time playing with my dad. Even as a little kid I could see how it brought us closer together. Just like every little boy, attention from my father made me feel strong and proud. I can't even begin to quantify how much that time meant to me.

That morning, I was thinking pretty deeply about all this and accidentally passed the path that led up a gentle hill to a park. Frankie called out to me.

"Daddy, the playground is that way," she said, pointing with her little finger.

She never misses a trick. There was no way she'd let me pass that turn. Not in a million years. Smiling, I backtracked and took her to the park. I was only halfway through my run, but I like nothing better than seeing my daughter play.

She pretty much jumped out of the stroller and headed for the little playground. She raced around, asking me to push her on the swings. I did. We played together for a good half hour. She started to slow down, and I realized my heart rate was still up.

"Let's keep going to the waterfall," she said at one point.

So she got back into the jogger, and we took off again. I passed her down a sippy cup of water, and she watched the scenery pass by as I ran back out to the path, my thoughts returning to my dad.

Things changed with him when I got a little older. He got busier. By the time I was in high school, he was spending longer and longer hours at work. At my games, I would look for him in the stands but he wasn't there.

It wouldn't be until years later that we reconnected, and we did it through sports. One of our favorites was squash. I'll never forget the first time I beat him and what that meant to our future games. It felt weird being better than my dad at something. If that feeling got to me and I started shaving off points, he'd get mad at me and tell me I was doing it on purpose. He let me know it was okay to claim a win, to enjoy it even.

From my dad, I learned how important play was to me. His ability to connect with me through sports really influenced my life. It's kept me in shape and let me chase my dreams. I'm really thankful to him for that.

At the same time, I think about that part of my life when he wasn't around as much. I missed having him there, and I don't want my daughter to have that feeling. I know how easy it is for life to get in the way (believe me, I feel it every morning at 6:30 AM), but I fight through it because that's how important Frankie is to me. That's the core of it; that's why I wanted to help write this book. It's a little inspiration for those of us who want more for our kids (and maybe a bit more for ourselves as parents, too).

It was at this point in my run that we reached the waterfall. I could feel the vibration in the handle of the jogger. Frankie was kicking her feet, getting excited. "Daddy," she called up to me. "Can I get out?"

"Sure," I said.

My run wasn't over yet, and I had my heart rate up nice and high. I was in the zone. But I stopped the stroller and helped Frankie get out. She was laughing, and the sound mixed with the patter of falling water. Frankie loves to get behind the jogger and push it, even though it's way more massive than she is. She did, and I walked along beside her.

"Let's all run," she said.

So we did. She started in that little pigeon-toed way she has, her blonde hair bouncing side to side. And I jogged alongside her, watching.

"You're a good runner," I told her.

"Thanks, Daddy," she said. "When I get bigger we can all run together."

"I can't wait," I said.

Right then, Frankie fell down. Her knee was skinned a little, but she didn't cry that much. I helped her up and asked if she was okay.

"I'm okay," she said. "I was going too fast."

"We all fall down sometimes," I told her. "We just have to get back up and keep going."

She looked up at me with a very serious expression. I could tell she was mulling it over in her own kid way.

"I'm going to run a little slower," she said. "Like this."

I could see her breathing getting faster and faster. Her face turned red, but she was having a blast being active and exercising, in her way, with Daddy.

Eventually she got tired, and I helped her back into the jogger. We finished our run, and she pretended to drive as I loaded up the stroller. Before I started the engine, I heard her sniffing softly in the backseat. I looked over my shoulder and saw her face all scrunched up. It's really cute when she does that.

"You stink, Daddy," she said to me.

Her words made me laugh. What a perfect ending to our morning.

I thought about everything that had gone through my head that morning—why I wanted to write this book, what it meant to me—and I thought about her simple statement. In a way, it was exactly why I've put my heart and soul into this, because the last thing Daddy wants to do is stink. All I think about is being the best dad I can be. And it was a hard-earned and deeply loved stink that morning, because it came from playing with Frankie.

Introduction | Mark Schlereth

I was lucky enough to play a game for a living, but I have been a parent for even longer. Twenty-four years and counting, as a matter of fact, and I will be until the day I die. I'm a kid at heart, and I needed that in my life. I can tell you, though, that had I sacrificed being an active dad in my kids' lives, I don't think I would have been the football player I was. Twelve years in the National Football League, suiting up for Pro Bowls, being a part of three Super Bowl championship teams—those things define my career. My relationships with Alex, Daniel, and Avery define me as a man.

When Mark and I first started to discuss working on a sports-related book together, we both agreed that it needed to be a unique project. As we started to think about what it could be, we found ourselves reminiscing on the impact sports has made on our lives, not as professionals but as fathers and sons. Sure, it's in our job descriptions to be obsessed with the action on the field, scores, and post-game analysis, but like most dads, my love of sports goes beyond that.

Mark Schlereth and family take in son Daniel's MLB game

I deeply believe that sports, or games in general, offer moments for us to let go and just play. In between the sweat, skinned knees, laughs, and bad calls, we learn things about ourselves and each other. These days, virtual sports now outshine Little League and other recreational sports. In a world dominated by video games, too many children spend hours on the couch. What hasn't changed is that every kid needs active play. For that to happen, we parents need to remember, and maybe even learn, how to play again.

The book you hold in your hands is your guide—a collection of personal stories from some of the biggest names in sports. These men and women have been role models for generations in this country because of their heroic feats on the field, in the ring, on the course, and on the court. What makes this book special is that we asked them to share a different sort of inspiration—stories of their lives as ordinary parents and kids, learning life's lessons through the simple act of play. Our hope is that this book will be the start of your own collection of stories. I know from my own memories that it's time well spent.

The other day I went into Avery's room. She's my youngest daughter. Considering the topic of this book, I'd like to say I was in there to spend some quality time with her, or even to play some practical joke, but it wasn't anything so interesting. I can't even remember why I went up there, but I was near her desk and I looked up to see a napkin tacked to her bulletin board. It made me smile.

See, I'd given her that napkin. Every morning that I can, I wake up half an hour before everyone else and make the kids' lunches. I always include a note on a napkin. It's a thing I've done since the kids were in elementary school, and it's something I still do. In school, it's a big deal. Avery tells me that a bunch of kids gather around at lunch to see what stupid quote or message I've left. My daughter particularly remembers the one I sent that read:

Dear Avery,

I remember when you were still a baby in Mommy's tummy. I wanted to name you Cockadoodoo Schlereth. But Mom decided to call you Avery Jordon. I guess that's okay. Study hard, like you always do.

Love, Dad

You have to understand that I know about all the kids reading it at school. I was going for shock value, man. Along with a joke or something to embarrass the kids in good fun, I always added some kind of encouragement.

Leaving those little notes means something to me. Seeing the note on Avery's board, I knew that those things mean something to her, too.

It got me thinking. I travel a lot, giving talks on success. Inevitably I get asked parenting questions. One of the most popular is how to spend "quality time" with your kids. This question makes me laugh. I think back to the times I've tried to schedule quality time with my kids. It usually ended up with someone getting upset, the kids fighting, and all of us driving home in a silent car.

Here's the trick I've learned—if you focus on *quantity time*, then quality time just happens. You can't force quality. Instead, you have to be there to grab that time and cherish it whenever it pops up. That's why I refused to let my kids ride the bus. Instead I drove them to school every morning. It's stealing time with them. And because they didn't have time to decompress on the bus ride home, I got to hear all their stories from the day. That is what this book is all about—seizing and creating moments.

Quantity time means getting up even when your mind or body doesn't necessarily agree. For me, the challenge was with my body more often than not. You see, football is a game played by warriors. Inevitably you get beaten up. You don't want to know how many surgeries I've had on my knees. That's another story for another day.

Believe me, there were times when I was playing football that all I wanted to do was sit in the ice tub a little longer or crawl into bed and sleep off the pain. When you are a dad, though, that's not an option. Nine times out of ten the ride home from practice wasn't the end to my day. It was the beginning of the real fun—playing with my kids.

It brings me back to when I was playing for the Redskins. At the time, I had two kids: my daughter Alex, who was about six, and my son Daniel, who was four. Often we'd have a Monday night game against the Cowboys, a typical NFC East brawl with our biggest rivals. The next Wednesday I'd be at practice all day. Because of the short week, our next game being on the following Sunday, it would be intense.

My buddy Mark Adickes and I would drive back to my house. I'd turn onto our street and see all the kids. There'd be about a dozen of them running around in my front yard. I could hear them even with the windows of the truck rolled up.

Alex was the elder statesman of the neighborhood back then. She'd run around back and reappear carrying a couple of Nerf archery sets. She'd hand them to us with this very serious face, and then all the kids would take off. They'd scatter as if they'd just broken a window playing stickball, literally tripping over each other trying to get around the side of the house to find a hiding place.

Sometimes, I'd get Mark—I know, another Mark—to set up an ambush. He'd climb up on the railing of the porch. It was surrounded by trees, so no one could see him. Then

I'd flush out the kids and run them around the other side of the house.

Half the time my buddy would let fly and hit me in the chest, totally missing the kids. I'd be in character, man. My legs would come out from under me. I'd clutch my chest, then fall on my back. Maybe I'd howl in pain.

Right about then, my wife usually stepped out onto the porch. She'd have one of those looks on her face—if you're married, you know the one.

"Come on in for dinner, *children*," she'd say.

Usually Alex would come up behind me and give me a big hug. I'd be aching pretty bad, but that would help with the pain.

For a second, I thought about what the evening would have been like if I hadn't seized the opportunity and remembered to play. I would have gone inside, lounged around, and packed my body in ice. My kids would have seen me as a football player in pain. Instead, they saw me as a fun dad.

When it came to spending quantity time with my kids, sometimes my aching body wasn't the only hurdle. I coached Daniel's baseball team for years. You might think that, being a pro athlete, it was totally natural for me to coach, but I knew nothing about the sport. Let me tell you how bad I was. I was sitting in the dugout one afternoon in the fourth or fifth season I'd coached. Not much was going on. The game wasn't one of those memorable ones. Not much drama to it. The kids were playing the field, and we were up by a few runs.

The Schlereth family

A kid from the other team was trying to bunt. He missed the first pitch. His second try went foul. Nothing special to that. But when the pitcher wound up for the third pitch, the batter squared off again.

I was in shock. I spun around.

"Hey!" I said to one of the other coaches. "That kid can't do that!"

The coach gave me one of those looks—not like the one my wife gives me. More like he thought I was either crazy or messing with him.

"What?" I asked.

I'll admit it. I honestly thought that you couldn't bunt with two strikes. Eventually, the other coach figured that out.

"You can bunt, but if it goes foul you're out," he said.

"Oh," I said, nodding.

Maybe I should have been embarrassed. Maybe I was. The funny thing is that wasn't the worst of it. No, that happened a few years later. It started out when my son ripped what should have been a stand-up double. The ball hit the wall on a couple of bounces. I was coaching first base at the time. Right away I noticed that my son was trotting around the base, admiring his work. I yelled for him to hustle, but it wasn't until he saw the center fielder glove the ball cleanly off the wall and throw a laser to second base that he started to pump those legs.

Needless to say, he was thrown out at second. It was the third out of the inning, and I met him halfway between first and second.

"That's unacceptable," I said to him. I might have been yelling just a little by then. "You didn't hustle."

I was on him all the way back to the dugout. For me, what he had done was the worst possible thing. He was good. I knew he was good, that he had real talent, and part of me wanted to make sure that people knew that his success came from his ability, not from the fact that his dad had been a pro athlete.

My son couldn't understand that. I know his teenage brain just didn't get it. But that didn't make it any better. When he got back to the dugout, he wasn't looking at me. Then he grabbed a Gatorade.

That's when I lost it. Like he needed a Gatorade! Like he was so tired from running his heart out on the base path!

I regret it now, but I slapped the Gatorade out of his hand and screamed at the top of my lungs. My wife appeared with tears in her eyes from having seen me lose my temper. She told me to leave, that I was embarrassing the family. So that's what I did, and just like that I was ejected from the game. Later on, my son came to me and said he understood where I was coming from. My wife was still right in kicking me out, but I think my son thought twice about dogging it after that.

Like I said, quantity time isn't always a walk in the park. Well, sometimes it is just that, but other times it can be challenging. I guarantee it won't always be perfect. But if you have enough of it, there will be some perfect moments, like that evening shooting neighborhood kids with Nerf arrows.

Now my son and I laugh about the whole Gatorade moment. My wife almost smiles about it, too—as long as we change the subject pretty quickly. Luckily, when you focus on that quantity time, it's always easy to come up with another good story on a dime if you have to.

That brings me back to the note tacked to Avery's board. I leaned over and read it that day, although I already knew what it said.

Dear Avery,
   Have fun at soccer. Run fast and play hard. You're the best little girl in the world.
   Love, Dad

I guess it's as simple as that.

Ready, Set, Play!

Parents and Children Bonding Through Sports

George and Monk Foreman | Boys and Their Toys

George Foreman is a two-time World Heavyweight Boxing Champion and an Olympic gold medalist. At the age of 45 he became the oldest man to win a heavyweight title. He is now a nationally recognized spokesman and minister, and is the father of 10 children.

George "Monk" Foreman III is George Foreman's second son. He is a graduate of Rice University, and he recently won his first professional heavyweight boxing fight.

George and Monk Foreman sat down to talk about education, boxing, practical jokes, and other interests that run in the Foreman family.

George Foreman: The best thing about being a dad is you have a purpose in life. You can't just roll over and quit. I've had things happen to me, hard things, and I've said, "It's enough." Then I look at my children and I realize they are dependent on me. I need to have the courage to be there with them, to play with them and teach them the rights and wrongs of life. So I just say, "I can live through this." You can lose an arm or a leg or a job, but when you're a dad, you still have a purpose in life. I wake up every morning and know I have to be a strong arm of guidance for my kids. Every kid needs that. But not every kid gets it.

My childhood started off without much guidance. My mom and dad broke up early, and my dad left. My mom tried to work two or three jobs. Her style was, "I'm gonna argue with you and fuss with you and make you straight, so that when I get home, you'll be alive one more day."

Now and then I would see my dad. Even though he had problems with alcohol, he shared some of the kindest moments of my childhood. They would be brief and there wasn't much play, but he'd put his hand on my head and encourage me. He even used to call me, "George Foreman, Heavyweight Champion of the World. Stronger than Jack Dempsey, hits like Jack Johnson."

I was just a kid. I didn't even know what that was, the heavyweight champion. I remember those moments, though. He would come in and out of my life briefly, but those moments always made me feel so good.

Monk Foreman: Some people look at being a father as, "I'm doing a great thing if I take care of my kids and I should get a medal." What I get from my dad is there isn't any other option. You have to be a *great* father.

GF: I didn't get to play much with my mom, either. She was busy, and I guess she didn't know better. That's not to say I don't have some nice memories, though. Those few moments she had for me stick to my mind like it was just yesterday.

She'd call me over.

"Come here, I want you to dance for me," she'd say.

She'd put music on, and I'd dance for her. I'd turn a flip. I'd do everything I could to show my mom I was a good dancer. She would clap her hands.

"Look at my boy dance. Look at that boy dance."

If you asked me what was the most playful moment of my life, it would be putting on a dance and turning flips for my mom. She made me feel like the most exciting dancer ever.

So when it came time for me to be a dad, I looked back at those moments. They helped get me ready. But there were other factors in my life that helped even more.

MF: I'd say my fondest memories of spending time with my father happened on the ranch. It was Dad around some cows and horses and grass. It stripped everything down to just a relationship between father and son.

GF: The Job Corps was really where I got my big break. When I enrolled, not only was I getting my vocation and basic education, but I met people who encouraged me. They were role models. One of the most important things I learned from being in the Job Corps was what a dad was supposed to be. I met people there who had families. Some of them would take me home and show me kindness. They would treat me real nice and let me spend time with their families.

One of those people was Charles "Doc" Broadus. It was February 1966 when he picked me out of a whole boxing team and, for some reason, just stuck with me. At the time, I didn't really want to be a boxer. I just wanted to be a street fighter. I wanted to go back home and beat people up. But Doc Broadus started talking to me about the Olympics, stories about Muhammad Ali, Joe Frazier. It turned me into a different fellow. He told me to stop fighting in the street so I could make a better person of myself.

It wasn't always easy for him, being there for me. I tell this story in church all the time. As the years went by, I left the Job Corps and went back home to Houston, Texas. I was about 17 and getting into trouble again. I'd lost the guidance of a father figure in my life.

Miraculously, Doc came to find me. He was not a wealthy man. But he used his paycheck to fly me back to San Francisco. Boy, did that get him in trouble with his wife.

"I don't know why you're spending that $85 on one of those kids," she said to him. "We could use that money. Why do you help those boys? They're never going to be anything. They're no good."

I can't blame her. She was right in a lot of ways. Doc was always helping kids, and they were always getting in more trouble. But he told me his side one day. He said, crying, "I had to help you. You were just as much a child of mine as any of my own."

He was the father I was looking for all those years, Doc Broadus. That's the great father image I have. He never treated me as less than his own children. Doc Broadus really loved me. And with that, he spent the time to show it.

I put it all together. If I ever had children, Doc had taught me what I needed to do. But the foundation came from my own mom and dad. The one thing I knew all along was that they really loved me. They just couldn't get it together. They really loved me, but they didn't spend the time. I didn't have the guidance. I didn't get to play with them.

When I had kids, I knew I was going to make it different for them. In life, there are so many things you can attach yourself to that aren't any good. I decided early on that I was not going to just talk to my kids. I would love them but also teach them by example. They would look at my life and know where to turn left, where not to turn right.

> *I decided early on that I was not going to just talk to my kids. I would love them but also teach them by example. They would look at my life and know where to turn left, where not to turn right.*

MF: My favorite thing about my dad is that he's always willing to take it to the limit with anything he does. No matter if it's training, writing a book, or being a dad. He really pushes things to the limit. There is no quit in him.

GF: Life is tough. Being Heavyweight Champion of the World is tough. Being an Olympic gold medalist is tough.

But life itself is really about the toughest thing you can ever know. To teach your kids, they have to see the same thing every day. They can't see a fellow who flip-flops through life, who falls down and doesn't get up. My kids have seen me fall. But they always see me brush my pants off, spit in my palms, and say, "Let's go."

One way to teach that lesson came naturally to me. It was through playing with my kids. Each one of my 10 can tell you the same story about a game called Bad Guy/Good Guy. George Jr.—he's about 33 years old now—he'd tell the younger ones that story. He'd tell them about how the two of us would be driving in the car and George Jr. would say, "Hey, Bad Guy." I'd turn into this monster, howl and roar. George Jr. would yell quickly, "Good Guy, Good Guy!" and I'd cut it off. I'd say, "Oh, hi, guy." Sometimes, he'd get nervous and mix up Bad Guy and Good Guy. That was when it got really funny.

When he'd tell the younger kids, they'd scream, "He did that to me, too." They've all had that experience with me. There were one or two who didn't get it. Monk, he just couldn't get it. Instead of saying "Good Guy," he'd get tough on me. Later, I'd try to explain it to him but he'd have none of it.

"You scared me," he'd say. "I had to defend myself."

I'd say, "No, man, you're just supposed to say, 'Good Guy.'"

It isn't just Good Guy/Bad Guy. I try to play as much now, with my 10th kid as I did with George Jr. Yesterday I got my youngest son up in the morning. He's George VI, but we call him Joe. He's nine. I got him on the bench press with light weights. He did his three sets. He got on his sit-up machine and he did his lunges.

Later on, I got talking to my wife.

"Boy," she said, "Joe's already been doing his Wii thing."

I said to myself, "Wii is still a video game."

There is no way you can compare that, sitting in a room playing by yourself, to being outside and exercising. You have to have real activity.

The activity level today is too low. Don't get me wrong: I love video games. I buy every new one that comes out. But I overload my kids with activities first. It's important as parents to do that. You can't just chalk it up to a change in the times. You have to have the courage to fight it for your kids' sake.

It might be harder for kids today to stay active, but it's nobody's fault. It's just the way of the world. Sometimes the wind starts to blow, and there is a dust storm. Who can you blame for a dust storm? No one. Sometimes you just have to wait for it to pass and then get all the dust off you.

It isn't always easy convincing the kids to get that dust off, though. Having children and doing it right takes time. And deep down, I know that all of us have the time. It reminds me of the old saying, "The only difference between men and boys is the price of their toys." Men are going to play; maybe [it's] poker with their buddies or golf with their friends. They'll always find the time.

Monk and George Foreman

GF: I learned, in raising children, I may as well spend that time playing with my kids. I found things that they liked. I didn't worry if it was too elementary for me. Whatever they were into, I would play with them, wrestle with them, get down on the floor with them, everything.

MF: My dad played basketball with us, but we tried not to box with him. He loves dominos, playing cards, and playing practical jokes. When he beats us, we hear about it for the next week. He'll tease, tease, tease. If he loses, he gets all quiet. He always finds a way to get you to play him again until he wins. He's slick like that.

GF: Even today, I will arm wrestle with my kids. We play dominos. And when I win, I boast like I just won the championship of the world. I get into games. Men are going to play anyway. We might as well play with our kids. That's been an important ingredient in my life.

Even with all that play, my kids know I'm a serious fellow. But like they learned from Bad Guy/Good Guy, I'm the biggest joker of all time, too. Sometimes they yell at me, "Dad, you play too much!"

That's when I know I've done something right. It's better to play too much than to not play enough.

MF: My dad loved to play practical jokes. He liked to take shaving cream and chase us down. If he caught one of us, he'd put it all over us. One night, everybody got in the room. We were hiding, waiting for him to come by so we could get him with shaving cream. As soon as he came, we busted the door open and scared him. He said, "Oh my God," and put his hands up on his chest like he was having a heart attack. Then he hit the ground and just laid there flat. He acted like he couldn't get up or do anything. We had to serve him dinner right there on the ground.

GF: Right from the start, sports have always been a big part of playing with my kids. I played basketball with all of them. I can play a half-court game with them now. But if they start dribbling, they lose me. I'll bump and snatch rebounds, though.

You have to play with your kids, even if it hurts. I remember when I was training for my boxing comeback. My oldest boy, George Jr., wanted to play basketball. So I went out and tried to jump and block his shot. I came down and popped my knee out. I had to snap it back together. I'm getting ready to fight Evander Holyfield, and I'm out there trying to get my son ready for basketball. I had to have surgery just before the fight.

At the same time, your kids might love what you love. I think it's wonderful that George III, we call him Monk, is a boxer. Just because he's in the "family business," though, doesn't necessarily make it any easier. It bothered me a little at first. But there's nothing better than doing something with your kids.

Monk will be the first to tell you that I forced all of them to get a college education before they did anything else. He graduated from Rice and got good grades. He started collecting for his master's classes. And then he decided he wanted to box. I think it's great. But I think all boxers should go to college first.

He said he started late. I said it was the right time. No one should pursue anything until they've pursued every opportunity they have for a good education. I left boxing a pretty wealthy fellow in the '70s and went through the '80s pretty good. Then I looked up one day and I was broke. I didn't want to be a boxer anymore. I was what, 40 years old? I wanted to do something else. But I was forced to go back to the most physical activity I knew to get myself back in shape and do something I didn't want to do because I didn't have the education to do something else.

All I needed at that time was a good profession. If I had just educated myself properly earlier on, I could have done that. In this life, you can lose a billion dollars more easily than you can $65,000. You need something to fall back on so you always have a way to help the community and your family. So I pressed those kids about education to no end.

MF: My father always put education first. He didn't graduate from school, and I think he wished he was a little more educated, that maybe if he had been he wouldn't have gotten swindled with his money the first time around. He wouldn't have had to go back to boxing. He could have been a professor. All he talks about is degrees. We didn't walk around the house seeing gold medals and trophies and belts. There were books everywhere, dictionaries and thesauruses.

We didn't walk around the house seeing gold medals and trophies and belts. There were books everywhere, dictionaries and thesauruses.

❧

GF: Whether it's boxing, basketball, or the world championship in dominos, you have to make the time. I knew my parents loved me, but there just wasn't time. When you come home, there is a sacrifice you have to make. It doesn't matter how many jobs you're working; you are going to find time somewhere to relax or go play with your friends. I've seen people working three jobs who still find two hours for bingo. Those hours you took for yourself, you have to take for your kids. You've just got to do it. There's always time.

Honestly, I think that some dads are scared to take that time. It takes courage to put yourself out there. The hardest

George Foreman Jr. (center) with sons George III (right) and George IV

thing about being a dad is knowing that your kids have to go through all the things you've gone through in life, and you can't stop it.

I was one of those guys who took my kids to first grade and cried. I knew what they were going to go through. There was going to be teasing; they were going to worry about homework. I cried each time because I realized that life is going to be rough for them. But they're going to have to live it. All I can do is spend as much time as I can with them and play with them, even if it drives them crazy. I'm pretty sure they'll thank me when the time comes.

It takes courage to be a dad, and it's never too late to find it. Even my dad learned that. When I was an adult, we reconnected. After I found my religion back in the '70s, I became a minister. My church had a lot of ministers, so I started preaching on the street. One particular corner I preached on was near the place where my dad got his beer.

He got to the point where he was so worried about me that he followed me to church. He even dressed up and came to the service. It took him a month to investigate, to see what was wrong with me. But about a year later, he realized there was something wrong with him, not me. So we became brothers in church.

I had four kids at the time. We never talked about what he and I missed out on, but it taught me a lesson about love. I was going to make certain that I wouldn't have to reconnect with my kids some day. I was going to keep that thing going from day one. I was going to hold them, hug them, spend time with them, and, most of all, play with them.

MF: With my dad, there was always too much of him to go around. When he'd leave town, we'd take a deep breath. I want my kids to get that same feeling that they can breathe when I leave. I don't want them to feel like they can't get me enough. I want them to feel like they're getting a little too much of me. That means when they go through tough situations, they'll know that dad is always in their corner.

GF: All your kids really need is you. Just a little hug now and then, a little holding of hands, and some time to play with you. They don't need video games and money. I still hold my big boy, who is now 33 years old. I grab him and hug him and hold on for a second. Hug your children. Don't be afraid. Dads need hugs, too.

Hug your children. Don't be afraid. Dads need hugs, too.

It takes a lot of courage to say, "I'm going to love my kids 100 percent, with every drop of my heart." I think back to my own dad. He finally got it straight. He finally found the courage to be a dad. And you know what? Because of that, he and my mom got to spend their last days on this planet together, and with me, as a family.

The lessons I learned from him and from Doc gave me the courage to put myself out there and love. Once I had that, playing was second nature. Now my kids can only say I've played with them too much. And that brings a big old smile to my face.

Grant Hill | Going the Extra Six Inches

Grant Hill is an NBA player with the Phoenix Suns. He won two NCAA Championships with Duke University. He was the first rookie to lead NBA All-Star fan balloting, and he won the NBA Rookie of the Year Award. He has two daughters.

My dad used to say that there are six inches between a pat on the back and a pat on the butt. That was the first thing my mind went to when I was asked to contribute my thoughts on parents playing with their kids. It's a great metaphor. Even though my generation's parenting style is different than his, it still applies. It's all about contact.

So when we started this process and I was asked a simple question, it took me a second to answer. The question was, "Do you have one story from your childhood that stands out when you think about parents playing with their kids?"

"Wow," is what I said. "There are a lot of stories."

For me, there were two things that made this question difficult to answer. One, my dad was a professional athlete.

He had a 12-year career as a running back, playing for the Dallas Cowboys, the Washington Redskins, and the Cleveland Browns. He was also the dad who would come out into the street and play with me and all the other kids in the neighborhood. He'd be the all-time QB when we played football. He was a great dad, and it was difficult for me to pick just one story. The second reason is because I am a dad now, too, and that's changed my perspective on a lot of things. But one thing runs true in both my life as the child and my life as the dad: it really is all about contact.

It really is all about contact.

When I was a kid, my dad and I would go out and have a catch. I loved throwing the football with him. He was a baseball player who was drafted out of high school, so I also loved going to the diamond and tossing the ball around.

I know it wasn't always easy for my dad. He was a busy man. But he found the time to be out there playing with me. It wasn't about a dad who was a professional athlete or a dad who was a Little League father; it was just a dad playing with his son.

The funny thing is that it wasn't always so easy for me, either. Obviously, his life as a professional athlete helped make me the man I am today. We were active together, and fitness was important. He taught me about sportsmanship and character. By example he showed me how to strive for the top, to be the best.

At the same time, that part of his life led to what little rebellion I mustered up as a teenager. I didn't dye my hair or get a tattoo. I was an only child and so were both of my parents, so we were always very close. My father went to Yale, and my mom was a successful businesswoman. When you have parents who are high achievers, you want to carve out your own niche and have your own identity.

I remember when I started to make a name for myself as a high school basketball player. I had been named the Northern Virginia Player of the Year, and colleges were starting to recruit me. I'd look for my name in the paper, and when I found it, the last name was always wrong. Instead of "Grant Hill," it read, "Grant Hill, son of Calvin Hill."

I don't even know if anyone realized it bothered me. But I wanted to make a name for myself at that point. I wanted to be just Grant Hill. I credit my dad, and the time we spent together when I was younger, in keeping that feeling in check with me. We'd built such a strong relationship through our time bonding and communicating over sports. He'd spent so much time with me, teaching me the importance of character and sportsmanship. Although part of my ego yearned to shine, I'd been raised better than to show that. Instead, I put my head down and tried harder. I used that success my father had as a guide, not a hindrance or a crutch.

I used that success my father had as a guide, not a hindrance or a crutch.

At times I was embarrassed a little bit because of my dad's success. Not everyone had that. Now that I'm older, I realize how lucky I was to have a dad who was so involved—a dad who came to soccer games and swim meets, stuff I know he'd have had no interest in if I hadn't been involved.

I know that the lessons my father taught me during our time playing together didn't just apply to sports. At the time, he didn't know that I would be a professional athlete. I'm sure he hoped I would be, but it wasn't about that. It was about raising a well-adjusted son who would give back to society and strive for success in whatever he chose to do. At the same time, a lot of our time playing together revolved around sports. We both loved it, so why would it have been any other way?

We still have that kind of relationship today. Being an athlete, he was great to have by my side while I went through the recruiting process, college, picking an agent, and entering the NBA. Through all the marketing opportunities, injuries, and free agency, the relationship we built playing together when I was a kid has always been a beacon that I use to guide my decisions. I have someone on my side who has been there and yet didn't want anything from me but my happiness. I'm very lucky.

Thinking back, I'll never forget the first time I beat him in basketball. I didn't have a big brother, so growing up it was all about getting big enough and good enough to beat my dad.

When it happened for me, I was in the eighth grade. My AAU team had just won the national championship, and I was getting serious about basketball. I was about 6'3½", around the same height as my dad. He had about 80 pounds of muscle on me, and up until then he had been taller and stronger than I was. He could do things on the court that I couldn't do.

When we went to the park and played one-on-one that day, I beat him pretty badly. I think it was 20–2. We played a second game, and I think that one also was 20–2. I didn't just beat him—I destroyed him. It was that time in my life. I was confident, and I'd just had a growth spurt. He's been ducking me ever since.

I didn't feel bad. I was proud. Growing up, I wanted to beat him. I wasn't a poor sport when I lost. And my dad wasn't the type who was hard on me or got physical. He might have gotten physical during that game, but not any of the others. The thing is, it was his support and love— and the time he spent with me—that let me feel that way. My dad knew competition, and he respected it. I think our relationship let him be as proud of me as I was of myself. That's what being a parent is about.

When it comes down to it, a lot of my memories are of learning the values that come from competition. It might have been a soccer match or a basketball game, a win or a loss. My dad was there for me to lean on and to talk through everything. It was great to have someone who'd been there and was older.

In the end, I made my own life. And every day I think about the time I played with my dad and the lessons he imparted to me. He taught me to be a man, to care for others and take pride in myself. He made sure I stayed active. To this day we have a real bond, the kind that grew from our time together—from constant contact.

❧

The second reason I found it hard to narrow down what I wanted to say about parents playing with their kids is that I'm a dad now. I realize I'm becoming my parents. It's depressing. (Just kidding.) But I am out there doing what my parents did, maybe even more. I feel like things have changed. If I don't go out with my daughters, they don't go out. My wife calls me Jack Brown, Richard Pryor's character in *Toys*. Part of it is that I'm a big kid myself. But it's more trying to encourage my kids so they can have fun like we did.

For my daughters, there isn't that luxury of, "Hey, Mom and Dad, I'm going outside." Nowadays kids can't be unsupervised, like we were when we were kids. These days kids can barely go out and ride their bikes by themselves.

I think that contributes to the childhood obesity issue. My mom gave me Coke and cinnamon buns for breakfast. But we went outside and played tag and kickball. Now in some communities, they don't have that luxury we took for granted. Maybe it's fear or maybe it's just not as safe, but the world has changed.

So I find myself outside with my daughters more, trying to play with them. That's not to say that I don't know firsthand how hard it is sometimes to get out there. We're in a world full of distractions, and the age of innocence is over. It can be hard at times to find the time. For me, during the season it's tough to get home as much as I'd like, but I make the time. Because at the end of the day, is there any better thing to make the time for than your kids?

During the off-season, I try to be Super Dad. People are always coming up to me asking, "Have you been at the beach?"

I say, "No, I was out playing with my kids and got all this sun."

One thing I've always done, even though it has caused trouble, is that if I am in town I take my older daughter to school, no matter what. I might have a game in Seattle on a Thursday night and then fly back, getting into Phoenix at 3:00 AM, but I'm up at 6:30 taking her to school. That's our time.

See, I want her to have an experience that's as close to what I had as a kid. I just try to teach her what I know. Sometimes she's absorbing things, sometimes she couldn't care less, but I never stop trying, even though times are so different from when we were kids.

There are more supervised play dates now. People are hiring personal trainers for their kids' sports! I'm dedicated to giving my daughters the good experiences I had, and the best way to do that is through playing together.

> *If I am in town I take my older daughter to school, no matter what. I might have a game in Seattle on a Thursday night and then fly back, getting into Phoenix at 3:00 AM, but I'm up at 6:30 taking her to school. That's our time.*

I try to take every chance I get. Our owner in Phoenix has a soccer field in his yard. He invites families over, and we play. This last time, I was out there playing with my oldest daughter. Although we were teammates, I could see her doing really well on her own and it made me feel good inside to see her from that perspective.

It was fun to participate in a sport together, even though it wasn't an organized "father-daughter" game. I'm so proud of her when she makes a save or punts the ball; it makes me feel better than anything I've accomplished because I think about the time I spent just kicking the ball around out back, helping her practice playing goalie, and I see the smile of pride on her face when she uses those skills. I helped her, and it made us closer for it.

It's important for me to remember that it's not about her being the best. It's not about her becoming a pro athlete. It's about her doing the best she can. Sometimes you learn more and grow more when you come in second place. That's what competition is all about. I don't care if she gets a scholarship. I don't even care if she's good. I just want her to learn and grow like I did.

Those moments of potential contact are out there every day. I take my daughter to tryouts and practice. Whatever she's into, it's important. I try to show her the world and expose her to things I was fortunate enough to be exposed to.

I have a funny story about that. One time, I did a commercial for a pool company. In it, I had to play with these kids who were actors. When my daughter saw the commercial on television, she got upset. She didn't want to share me with those kids.

It's a good example of how small a little kid's world is. But it was great to see that I was such a big part of her world that she didn't want to share me. It was an affirmation to me that I'd spent the time with her—that I had made the contact.

❧

After I processed the contact I'd had with my dad and the contact I have with my daughters, a story came to mind that surprised me. My childhood was filled with playing ball in the street with my dad. Now I'm always outside

Myla and Grant Hill in 2004

running around with my daughters. Considering that, it's funny that my mind focused on a story that seemed more like the end of my childhood. At the same time, it touched on everything I value about the relationship between a dad and his kids. The story was sort of a defining moment in the Hill household.

It was a hot August day. I was in middle school, which was right next to the high school. My dad drove me over to play some tennis.

First off, I think that my dad and I playing tennis together is the perfect story for this book. Neither one of us could play. We were out there thinking we could play. But we couldn't. Being a pro athlete, I'm sure it didn't sit great with my dad, playing a sport he had not perfected. But he was out there for me, making that contact with his son.

It was really hot, and the football team was outside practicing. I played a lot of football when I was a kid but never on an organized team. My dad had a rule that I wasn't allowed to play on a team until I started high school. He didn't want a Pop Warner father thinking he was Vince Lombardi and teaching me bad habits. Dad took his football very seriously. He didn't play until he was in high school. He figured that at 14 my body would be more developed and I'd have a coach who would teach me the right way to play.

For me, football was always my first love. I played all the time in the neighborhood. I grew up on the NFL sidelines, going to Cleveland Browns games as a kid. Football was my life.

Right then and there, in the scorching heat at the tennis court of the high school, I said, "Dad, I'm not going to be out there next year playing football. It's too hot. I'm going to be in the air conditioning playing basketball."

There I was, telling him I wasn't planning on following in his footsteps. I was kidding about the air conditioning but apparently not about the basketball. It must have disappointed him, but he never showed it.

> Right then and there, in the scorching heat at the tennis court of the high school, I said, "Dad, I'm not going to be up there next year playing football. It's too hot. I'm going to be in the air conditioning playing basketball."

My dad was out there playing tennis with me. He couldn't play a lick. He was just out there because I wanted to play. That time wasn't about making me into a football player or, thank heavens, into a tennis player. It was about being there for me and with me. It was about contact.

The bottom line is that regardless of what income bracket you're in and what resources you have or don't have, the most important thing is the time you spend with your kids. Your kids are your legacy—more so than what you do in business or in the community or in sports. And it's not just about your kids following in your footsteps. Ultimately, if you raise well-adjusted kids who have character and are respectful, you've made a difference. It might be a little more than six inches from the couch to get up and play with your kids, but it's worth it.

Julie Foudy | Glittery Pink Soccer Balls

Julie Foudy is the former captain of the U.S. Women's Soccer team. She is a three-time Olympic medalist and a two-time World Cup champion. After 17 years playing with the U.S. National Team, she was inducted into the U.S. National Soccer Hall of Fame in 2007.

The other day I went clothes shopping for my kids. I have a daughter, Isabel, and a son, Declan. I was looking for sports-themed pajamas. That's where the problem started.

I began the search with Declan. The boys section had what seemed like an unlimited supply. There was a brown pair with a baseball and bat. There was a yellow and black soccer-themed pair. There was the red, white, and blue basketball all-star pair. I had no problems finding ones for him.

Then I wandered over to the girls' section. First off, everything was pink and/or purple. I like pink, but something was missing. I could not find a single pair that had a sports theme. I found butterflies, fairies, and cute little bubble letters, but that wasn't what I was looking for.

It got me thinking. Why can't anyone make a pair of pink girls' pajamas with glittery soccer balls on them? It may be that I am shopping in the wrong stores, but I cannot find them. If I could, I would definitely invest in a few pairs.

I've noticed a similar thing when I am looking for toys. There seems to be more aisles of toys for boys than girls, and most of the girls' toys have something to do with kitchens or vanities. On the boy's side, everything is balls and trucks.

Not long ago, my husband came home with a pink kitchen set for Isabel. After one look I said, laughing, "Great, next you are going to bring home an ironing board."

I am not going nuts about this. I know I can buy my daughter a pink soccer ball. I am conscious of giving my daughter things like bats and balls so she knows there are options. That is important to me.

> *Not long ago, my husband came home with a pink kitchen set for Isabel. After one look I said, laughing, "Great, next you are going to bring home an ironing board."*

Growing up, I played with boys. That's how my soccer career began. It was the first grade, and I was at recess. I was six, and the boys would come and get me every day to play with them. One day after school, I asked my mom if she would sign me up to play on a team. At the time, I was too young. I had to wait a year.

I got to play on my first team when I was seven. It was the earliest I could. I played for a year and got selected to join a club team. Now club teams

Julie Foudy

are everywhere, but back then there were not as many. It was one of the first competitive clubs in Southern California. The weather was so nice you could play year round. At the time I didn't even know what a club team was, but they had green uniforms. And I liked that.

I played for that club team for eleven years. Back then, soccer was not that big. There are women a couple of years older than I am who say that soccer wasn't a part of their generation. I say, "What?" But it is probably true. I really timed it perfectly. Or I guess my parents did.

In addition to soccer, I played pretty much everything I could think of. I loved tackle football with the boys. I was a huge tomboy. I loved basketball, even though I never played it organized. I had a neighbor who was 6'5". We used to beat each other up under the rim. I played volleyball, softball, and track. I liked soccer and track the best.

Considering what women who are older than I am say about their opportunity to play sports, you might be surprised to hear that I never felt any added pressure or challenge because I was a girl. I didn't know what Title IX was when I was younger. Maybe it was because I had older brothers. Maybe it was because of my parents. All the times I came home all scraped up from playing tackle football, I cannot remember my parents every saying, "Honey, that's not something a girl should do." It was more like, "Whatever. Did you tackle any of the guys?"

> *All the times I came home all scraped up from playing tackle football, I cannot remember a single time that my parents said, "Honey, that's not something a girl should do."*

Maybe it was being the youngest of four. My sister was athletic, too. She gravitated more toward individual sports, like tennis and rowing. She played a little bit of soccer, but she was in many ways the same.

The only thing I remember is when I was playing football with the boys and a new set of boys came around, my buddies would say, "Yeah, you don't want the girl." They would sandbag it so they could get me on their team. I would play along. I found it funny—especially when I beat them.

The first time I remember really facing a barrier in sports came when I was in college. I studied abroad and went to Barcelona. I was training over there, running, but the women there didn't play soccer, not in the early '90s. In Spain, it was a man's sport.

One of my friends was over there with me who also played on the Stanford University women's soccer team.

We jumped into a pick-up game on the street. The game just stopped.

The guys were like, "Who are you? What are you doing? How can you play soccer?"

That was the first time I was exposed to how the game was so different for women globally. In the States, everyone grew up playing, girls and boys. I remember thinking, "Wow, what is the big deal?" I was flabbergasted.

Like I said, I do give a lot of credit for my outlook on sports to my parents. I like to call them Fruity Judy and Slim Jim, and they are classic—definitely not the parents of today. They weren't very hands on. While being hands off, though, they managed to be very supportive. They had no clue about soccer, which I think was a good thing. They would just stand on the sidelines and cheer me on. In every part of life, they encouraged me to do what I wanted to do. They didn't tell me to focus on this or focus on that.

"It is up to you, hon," they would say. "It is your decision. Ultimately, you have to live with it."

When I was a senior in high school, I had the chance to start on the national team. The team was going to Italy for a tournament, and it happened to be during my graduation. I had to make a choice—miss graduation and go to the tournament, or go to graduation and possibly miss out on becoming a starter on the U.S. team.

I went to my parents to ask their advice. Nowadays, I think I could predict a parent's response. He or she would say it is a no-brainer, of course you should go to the tournament. My parents, on the other hand, said, "What do

Julie Foudy and family

you want to do, hon? You are the one who is going to have to live with the decision."

I decided to go play. I earned the starting spot and missed my graduation. It was my decision, though, so I had no regrets. When it came time for me to make those tough decisions, like playing for the national team or going to prom, or playing in Italy or attending my graduation, they were just supportive and let me be who I was going to be, which was so critical to my development. They were not living vicariously through me. They were happy with whatever I chose to do in life. I think making choices like that prepares a kid for life as an adult.

That may, unfortunately, be very different from parents today. I hear about how the climate has changed for youth sports. The grassroots side of it is gone. For the national team I played on, all the kids played different sports. Soccer was one of them, but I didn't focus on it until I went to Stanford. At that point, the decision to forego other sports was more a matter of not having enough time.

Now parents are being told that their children have to focus on a single sport. That is a different pressure—not just on the parents, but on the kids, too. Everything seems ramped up. I never experienced that. I think I was fortunate.

This crosses over to things outside of sports. Being a parent today, I find it can be a hard balance. You want to push your kids in the right direction. You want to be hands on in a good way and curious, interested, and engaged. At the same time, you have to let the tether go a little bit and let them find their own way.

I hesitate mentioning letting the tether go. It could be an additional excuse for not spending time with your kids. There is no excuse for that. Parents, you have to get down on the ground and get dirty with your kids.

My parents were not living vicariously through me. They were happy with whatever I chose to do in life.

You have to get down on their level. Thankfully we have carpet in our living room, or I would have sore knees and elbows.

As the kids get older, another challenge I can see is making sure my kids have time to play. So much of a kid's life nowadays is structured. I want to make sure I leave time to spend at the park or in the backyard, just playing. I look at some kids in elementary school, and the parents are driving them from piano to Spanish lessons to art class. It is like they go from one thing to the next all day. When is there time for a kid just to be a kid? I spent hours a day playing as a kid. And I turned out all right.

As a parent, I struggle with not allowing myself to schedule everything for them. Work is part of it. As a mom, I want to be task-oriented when I am with the kids. I want to get the laundry done or the house cleaned while I am with them. Sometimes I have to just shut off the BlackBerry or postpone the errands and just set aside an hour to just focus on play.

As a mom, I want to be task-oriented when I am with the kids. I want to get the laundry done or the house cleaned while I am with them. Sometimes I have to just shut off the BlackBerry or postpone the errands and just set aside an hour to just focus on play.

I am constantly reminding myself that I don't have to be folding laundry while I am down playing with them. That is hard to do sometimes.

What I do is consciously take that hour. Lately I find myself saying, "Man, I should go through that mail," or, "Let me check one thing on the BlackBerry." Then I stop and tell myself that those things can wait. It is something I go in phases with. I made it my

New Year's resolution this year to find that focus on just playing and having fun.

I think it may be different for dads. My husband and I have this debate all the time. When I come back from traveling after he's had the kids, the house is not always perfect, but the kids look like they have had a blast. He will say, "I can't do both things. I'm watching the kids. Women are better multitaskers."

I think that might be an excuse, maybe something in the guys' guidebook. Looking at it the other way, though, he is much better at locking in and playing. I once heard a woman give a speech and she said, "Mess has no emotional content. It is not going to care if it is left alone for long periods of time."

That is something I struggle with. So what if the house is a little messier? So what if the dishes aren't done? I was looking at photos the other day and I said, "Gosh, they have already grown up so fast." I have to take advantage of it while they still want to play with me.

Most people think that dads play a little differently, too. They play a little more physically, but in my house it is pretty equal. Typically, it depends on the family. If it is a situation where the mom works, the kids become the mom's focus when she gets home because she hasn't seen them all day. If I have the kids most of the day when my husband is away, though, my play is more task-oriented. I might start them off, but then I move on to doing a chore. But if I have been on the road and my husband has had them for a while, I am totally focused on them. I think it is less gender-specific and more about the roles in your particular family—who is the primary caregiver and who is the one away from the house more.

Regardless of who is in charge, I think kids are less active nowadays. The obvious culprit is the video game. But there seems to be a heightened fear of negative things in life. I walked about five miles to school every day. In elementary and junior high, I walked it alone. I do not think that would happen today. I have memories that I was always outside with the neighbors. I do not get the sense that happens anymore.

With my kids, they are still so young. But I have a constant internal debate. Is the danger actually worse, or do we just know about it more? With the Internet and immediacy of the news, is it worse or is it just a heightened awareness?

The fact is I don't think I will let my kids walk as far alone as I did as a child. So even though my kids are one and three, it affects me, as well. I still think I would be fine if they dropped down to a neighbor's house for a few hours. I used to go down to the school and shoot soccer balls against the wall for hours. My parents didn't know where I was. I loved it. To be honest, though, I won't let my kids do that.

So how do we make sure our kids stay as active as we were? Again, the obvious answer is limiting video games and computers. It is going to be a part of their lives. I see that. But I cannot see them sitting in front of a screen all day. That would drive me nuts. I say that now, but parents of older kids are probably reading this and saying, "Yeah, easier said than done, babe."

I want to get my kids involved in organized sports at an early age. I want them to try a lot of different things. I think that was such a gift in my life—to be active, outside, and running around. So I'll get them involved and help them find what they love. I get a sense that both of my kids are naturally active. I do not see that as being a problem. Honestly, I cannot see my three-year-old being a pianist.

One great way to ensure that your kids stay active is to be active yourself. I remember the vacations I took with my family. They were fun, and they were very active. It wasn't strange that Mom went out running. When my son sees me put on my running shoes, he asks if he can go with me. Sometimes you get older, and life gets busier, and that gets lost.

Another great way to be involved is to get them into sports. For you dads out there, please don't hesitate to teach your daughter to catch. Kick a ball around with her. Even if she loves her pink kitchen set, sign her up for soccer.

> *One great way to ensure that your kids stay active is to be active yourself…. Sometimes you get older, and life gets busier, and that gets lost.*

Growing up, I never dreamed that one day I would be inducted into the U.S. Soccer the Hall of Fame. It didn't exist when I was a kid. Neither did the women's national or Olympic teams. There was no such thing. We pioneered a lot of that stuff.

It is such a cool feeling to know that kids could now have that dream. That is what I am most proud of, the legacy we left, that group of us.

When Mia Hamm and I found out we were inducted, I don't think I even knew I was up for consideration. I thought you had to be out longer. Mia and I laughed and said, "Are we that old already?" I think it was four years. It was a tremendous honor, though. It is hard to get into the Hall of Fame, and to get in on the first ballot with Mia was a huge honor. After everything the game had already given me, to be inducted along with one of my best friends, someone I had played with for about two decades, and to be mentioned along with the greats of the game in this country, it was incredible.

The goal of kicking a ball around with your daughter does not necessarily have to be that lofty—although all the power to her if it gets to that point. Sports can be invaluable to a girl for other reasons, too. Girls can be very awkward at 13. I remember looking back and seeing how awkward I was. Sports are what gave me confidence. I have always felt that soccer taught me every lesson in life. I learned it on the field from playing with teammates, from losing and from winning. I learned so much on the field that applied to life, and I didn't even realize it at the time.

> *I learned so much on the field that applied to life, and I didn't even realize it at the time.*

That is why I started the Julie Foudy Sports Leadership Academy. It is a week-long residential camp for girls 12 to

18 years old. It focuses on sports and leadership. The key to the academy is our effort to take girls in those teenage years and teach them not only to lead in sports but to lead in life.

The Leadership Academy is about how sports can teach you everything. On top of the health and wellness benefits, I think it is so important in every aspect of life. So when people ask me if my kids are going to play soccer, I say, "I don't know what they will play, but they will play sports." I will try every one until I find one they love. I want them to get those lessons in life. Sports are huge for character building.

My kids are one and three years old. I don't know what they love yet, but they will play something. Looking at them now, I don't think that is going to be a huge challenge. The other day, a boy down the street was out shooting baskets. He's eight. He asked Isabel if she wanted to play with him. I let her go over, and I watched as he tried to teach her how to shoot a basket. He was so patient and a great little instructor. After giving her a series of pointers and acting out the perfect shot, he handed Isabel the ball. She promptly drop-kicked it into the garage door. He gave it back to her, along with a calm explanation of the correct form. She drop-kicked it again. Maybe the apple didn't fall too far from the tree.

Watching my son, he likes to hit stuff. He'll pick up a stick and pound on a ball. As I watch my mind starts to turn. Maybe he'll like baseball or golf, or maybe hockey.

The other day I went as far as asking Isabel what she wanted to be. Was it a baseball player? Soccer? No, she said she wanted to be a princess. The next day, I tried again. Doctor? Nah, a princess. Maybe it is those pajamas. I just hope she grows up to be a pink princess who can beat all the boys at football!

Lou and Skip Holtz | A Pep Talk for Parents

Lou Holtz is one of the most successful college football coaches of all time. He led four different programs to top-20 finishes and six different programs to bowl games. He won a national championship while he was coach at the University of Notre Dame. A successful author and motivational speaker, he joined ESPN as a college football analyst in 2005. In 2008 he was inducted into the College Football Hall of Fame. He is the proud father of four.

Skip Holtz is Lou Holtz's son and the head coach of the University of South Florida football team. He has also been the head coach at East Carolina University and the University of Connecticut. He lettered in football at the University of Notre Dame and is the father of two sons and a daughter.

L ou and Skip Holtz talk about how they have both juggled coaching and parenting.

Lou Holtz: I'm known for my pep talks. Here's one for all you parents out there. There is no greater responsibility

The Holtz family circa 1974

than being a parent. You made the decision to have a child. You made the decision to make that child successful. There is nothing more important. A lot of people went into burning buildings on 9/11 to save lives. You are trying to save a life every day. You are trying to save a child. I don't know a more awesome responsibility than being a parent. It isn't always easy. Your kids will test you. And that's when your responsibility is at its greatest. Often your kids need your love the most when they deserve it the least.

One last thing. Don't live your life vicariously through your kids' experiences. So many parents do that because they failed at something when they were little. Let your children lead their own lives.

No matter how you look at it, everything starts with family. These are the people we lean on, and these are the people to which we are responsible. Without them, we would not be here. With them, we are all stronger for it.

Skip Holtz: If I could give any advice, it would be to spend time with your kids. Walk in the door with a smile on your face and set aside special time each day to be with them. I look at my 16-year-old. [Children] grow up so fast, and you cannot turn back the clock. Try to cherish each stage. I was not a fan of the infant stage. I could never tell if they wanted to be fed or changed or what. When I look back, I wish I had spent more time with them during that stage. Now it is about finding something that they like and doing it with them. I tried to get them into golf, but they didn't like it. They like to water ski and wakeboard. So now I drive the boat. I'd rather be golfing, but I know that the time with them is priceless.

LH: It was during my father's time in the service that I really learned how important family is. When he went overseas, my mother moved us from West Virginia to Ohio to be closer to her parents. She had three brothers. Two were in the service. The third, my uncle Lou, was in high school. He became my father, my brother, and my best friend. I confided in him. There was no one I valued more. I remember he used to take me down to the corner to see war movies. He had a great sense of humor, too.

"At dinner tonight, after your grandpa says something, tell him, 'That's propaganda,'" he told me one day.

I said, "What's propaganda?"

"It'll be funny," he said.

That night at the dinner table, Grandpa said something. I spoke up just like Uncle Lou told me to.

"That's propaganda," I said.

Grandpa hit the ceiling.

"You said it would be funny," I said to Uncle Lou later.

He smiled and said, "I thought it was."

Eventually Uncle Lou went into the service, too. He served for six months, and then the war ended. He liked to say it ended because of him. After he got out, there was the 52-20 Club. For veterans looking for work, they would receive $20 a week for 52 weeks. Uncle Lou applied to be the president of the local steel company or the elevator operator of a one-story building. My grandpa got mad because Uncle Lou was living off the government and kicked Lou out of the house. He came to live with us, and we just got closer. When I was coaching at Notre Dame, he only missed one game.

One of my fondest early memories of playing as a kid came from Uncle Lou. He bought me a cheap little football. This was during the Depression, so any ball or toy was a real treat. At the time, I didn't know much about football, but I remember playing touch football in the street. I was young, around five. The first time I got the ball, I ran away from everyone back toward my own end zone. I thought the game was really hard until I learned I could throw it over everyone's head.

Just like no one told me I could throw the ball at first, no one tells you how to be a dad. Deep down, you just want to be better than your own dad. When I was a kid, we were poor. There was no welfare or food stamps. I found out it wasn't what you had but *who* you had. Once we moved to Ohio, I had aunts and uncles who became a part of my life. For my kids, though, it was different. I preached to them that we wouldn't be around family like I was. I made sure they understood that they had each other. They had to learn to count on each other.

The lesson stuck. We still get together every summer for a week in July. All the grandkids, kids, and their spouses show up. I tell them it is mandatory if they want to stay in the will. We play golf in the morning, head home for a sandwich, then do something with the children in the afternoon and after dinner. At 9:00 we put the kids to bed and have a family meeting. One night we talk about the family business. The next, we talk about the foundation. Then we discuss religion and problems anyone is having. It ends by 11:00, although the kids have been known to keep talking until 2:00 in the morning. We stay close. I feel blessed. They are all happily married, they all have good lives, and they are still a family. That's what it is all about.

SH: I left my head coaching position at Connecticut when my mom got sick. A lot of people questioned my decision to go back to being an assistant. At the time, my wife said, "Will you regret you and the kids not being with your mom 20 years from now?" I would have. So we moved down to Columbia. I wanted my kids to know their grandmother, and we were blessed when she recovered. Since then, I've had people ask if I have regretted that decision. I honestly can say that I do not. I went there to spend time with my parents, and my kids spent their first six years of life with their grandparents. That is what life is all about.

LH: A family is not a family without responsibility. Considering my career, I think of it in terms of football. Coaching is not so different from parenting. I was responsible for those kids out on the field, and I took that very seriously.

I coached like I tried to parent, and I tried to parent like I coached. As a parent, you have to serve as a role model. You have to have standards and not worry about being popular. As a coach, I never worried whether the kids liked me or not. I had an obligation to make them the best they could be and prepare them for life.

Today, especially among single parents, too many people worry about being liked. The only person I worry about liking me is my wife. Instead, I focused on three simple rules: do the right thing, do the best you can, and show people that you care. It is the same for kids and players.

> *I focused on three simple rules: do the right thing, do the best you can, and show people that you care.*

At home, we always gave our children responsibility. A list of chores hung on the refrigerator, and the kids were expected to contribute to the welfare of the family. What they did, however, was their choice. If they chose not to

The Holtz family, present day

contribute, then they chose to stay in on the weekend. They would complain when the weekend came.

"I'm going out," one would say.

"You can't," I'd say. "You didn't do your chores."

When they protested, I'd say, "You chose to stay in on the weekend. I hope you don't choose that again."

I learned this lesson in the army. Life is a matter of choices, good or bad. We are all responsible for our actions. So if your child is sitting on the couch playing video games all day, that is your responsibility. If I let all those kids who played for me do whatever it was that they wanted to do, I doubt I would have coached for long. The responsibility to get them fit, in shape, and ready to play fell on my shoulders. As a parent, the same responsibilty falls on your shoulders when it comes to your kids.

When it comes right down to it, we as parents have two primary responsibilities. One is to do what we can to make sure our kids are safe. The second is to make sure our kids are as successful as they can be. Although safety seems like the harder of the two, success is far more complicated.

For me, it started with work ethic. I grew up during the Depression. My dad worked all the jobs he could when he wasn't in the service. I made sure my kids learned the value of work at an early age. Every one of them got their working permits at 15 or 16. They had to work for the summer. I tried to get them to take jobs at McDonald's, Wendy's, or the drug store. I wanted them to see how mean customers were to the people working behind the counter. They also had to save half of their salary. It helped teach them not to waste money.

I have been fortunate enough to lend a helping hand to my grandkids, too. We have a trust set up to provide for their education. There are some requirements. Definitely no drugs. When they are around 15, they have to spend one week per year with my wife and me. My wife did things with them during the day. At night, I talked to them about our family. My father was in the navy during World War II, but he never spoke about his time in the service. I was fortunate, thanks in part to being a coach, that a man who served with my dad contacted me. He had kept a diary and mailed it to me. I learned that my father served at Iwo Jima and Midway, and I want the kids to know the sacrifices that went into making this country great. I am not going to leave their education in the hands of college professors only. They need to learn from their family. You can't underestimate the importance of family.

SH: I would never say I am a better dad than my dad was. He was on the road a lot, at the office a lot. He was not around as much as he would have liked. But I understood the job he was doing. It was not like he was at the pub. He worked hard and taught us valuable lessons with his work ethic and the way he did things. Now it has changed. Because of the new NCAA recruiting rules, we can only go out in December and January. It has made it easier to be a parent, to give the kids that quality time.

> *I am not going to leave their education in the hands of college professors only. Children need to learn from their family.*

LH: When I was asked about how important play is to children, I thought about my kids and how they are such great parents. My dad wasn't perfect. I wasn't a perfect dad, either. I played with my kids, but not as much as Skip and Kevin play with theirs. Some of my favorite memories, though, are the times I spent with my kids when they were little. Sometimes the coach in me came out. I remember taking Skip and Kevin out before they started Little League. I'd throw a tennis ball for them to hit. Sometimes I'd throw it inside. I thought it was important for them to learn how to get out of the way.

When Skip was eight, I took him to his first Little League game. He came up to bat. The pitcher was probably 12 years old and about 6'2". The first pitch, a fastball, hit Skip right in the face. There was blood everywhere. I had to take him to the emergency room and then call his mother. I guess that lesson about getting out of the way didn't stick.

It was a different time, though. We didn't play with our kids like adults do, and should, today. But I remember spending a lot of time with them. When I was coaching at Ohio State, I took Luanne and Skip to the office one Sunday night. At the St. John Arena, the floors were linoleum and outside my office was a long hallway. My kids found a chair with wheels. Skip sat down and Lou Ann pushed him down the hall. They were screaming and having fun, but I didn't notice.

At the time, I didn't know [head coach] Woody Hayes was in his office next door. He came out.

"Who the hell's kids are making so much noise?" he yelled.

I stuck my head out. "Mine."

Woody looked at me and said, "God, they're healthy."

LH: Play is so important to children. There is no doubt that it helps keep them healthy, but it is also how they learn so much of what will make them the adults they are to become. Intermingled with that are your kids' friends. You cannot underestimate the influence they have. At the same time, friends can also be a great tool for getting a message across to your kids.

With a football coach for a dad, my kids faced some hurdles when it came to making friends. Whenever I think about how much we moved around, I go back to the trampoline. It was the first thing off the truck. We would put it up right in the front yard. Then they would unload all the furniture. Before we went to bed that night, our kids would know every other kid in the neighborhood. At first they thought moving was unfair, but through playing on that trampoline they learned to make new friends. That experience helped them as adults.

SH: I have a lot of stories about our trampoline. By stories, I mean split heads and bloody noses. It was a centerpiece to our moves. Today it would be different. Back then, all the kids were outside. They would see the trampoline and come over. Now everyone is inside playing video games. Back then, even my mom and dad would come out and get on the trampoline. It was a great way to meet the neighbors.

Whenever I think about how much we moved around, I go back to the trampoline. It was the first thing off the truck. We would put it up right in the front yard. Then they would unload all the furniture. Before we went to bed that night, our kids would know every other kid in the neighborhood.

LH: I always wanted my kids to bring their friends around the house. In the basement we had a bumper pool table, Ping-Pong, and a pinball machine. Our house was a place where the neighborhood kids would come and hang out. I liked it that way. To me, it was better than having the kids out at their friends' houses all the time. With my schedule, I never would have seen them if that had been the case.

Having all those kids playing in the house, I saw it as a chance to coach, too. We always tried to compliment the other kids on qualities that could be acquired.

"Oh, you have such good manners," we'd say to one of the kids' friends.

We'd never tell any of them they had beautiful eyes or comment about a quality that could not be learned. We saw it as a chance to help our kids grow. It had a very positive effect, and they barely noticed we were doing it because they were having fun playing with their friends.

That is not to say that direct communication with your children is not important, no matter what you are doing with them. When Skip and Kevin were little, I took them to a Pittsburgh Pirates game. By the second inning, they could spot a vendor eight sections away. After I'd gotten them one of everything already, I made a deal with them.

"I'll tell you what we'll do," I said. "If Pittsburgh wins, I'll buy you two anything you want."

They cheered. They paid attention to the game. When the Pirates' Roberto Clemente singled to win the game, they were so excited. They picked out a couple of souvenirs, and they still talk about that game to this day. If I had gotten angry at their behavior earlier in the game, none of us would even remember the day.

SH: Dad had a way about him. The times you would expect him to get the maddest, he was the most compassionate. He held us to very high standards; he expected a lot of us. Sometimes we would do something that didn't seem like a big deal, but he would get upset. When I really messed up, when I really thought I would get it good, he would look at me and say, "Is that the best you can do?" I would say,

"No, I can do better." My mother, on the other hand, was worse. I never saw her lose her temper or raise her voice. When I did something wrong, she would cry. I would say, "Punish me, ground me! Anything but that!"

LH: Now as to our other responsibility as parents. What good is teaching your children to be successful if you do not first keep them safe? Although we do not always want to think about it, life has its darker moments, too. Communication is important for teaching about the pitfalls of life. I always worried about drugs. I experienced drugs when I was a kid—I was drug to church, drug behind the wood shed, and drug to the sink to get my mouth washed out with soap. I didn't turn my back on the dangers for my kids, though. I told them that I never met a single person who claimed they succeeded in life because of drugs and alcohol. I've only heard the stories about how drugs and alcohol had ruined their lives.

At the same time, my wife and I let the kids be kids. Sometimes they had to make a mistake before they could learn. When we moved to a new town, we usually bought a new house. When we arrived in Ohio, it was no different. We bought a home in a neighborhood that was still being built. One night after I came home from the office and sat down to read the paper, my daughter found me.

"Dad," she said. "Do we have a ladder?"

"No," I said.

"Do you know where I can get one?" she asked.

I was suspicious at this point. "Why do you need one?"

"We need to go down the chimney of the house next door," she said.

"Why?" I asked.

"To get Kevin. He fell down."

I couldn't believe it. The poor kid had skinned up most of his body. One thing I had learned through life, though, was what I said in my pep talk. Children need love and understanding the most when they deserve it the least. Most of the time when they do something wrong, your first reaction is to get angry. It is better to wait until you have calmed down and then talk to them about it. You don't know what they went through at school, what disappointments or arguments they had that day.

What kids need to learn during those hard times is perseverance. It makes me think about my wife. When I was young, I didn't think about becoming a coach. I just wanted to work in the mill, have a car and a girl, and have five dollars in my pocket. I was a poor student but not dumb. I would have cruised through if it wasn't for the coach of my football team. He left school to take a job with the second-best team in the state. He told my mom and dad that I should go to college and become a coach. My mom and dad agreed with him. I didn't want to. But we compromised, and I went to school.

To pay for it, my mom went to work as a nurse's aide. At the time, if your dad paid taxes in the state, you were entitled to one free semester of school. That's how I got to Kent State. I loved history, so I thought I'd teach history in high school. When I graduated, I went into the Army. I learned more there than any other time in my life.

Out of the Army, I was offered a graduate assistant position. At the time, I was seeing my future wife, Beth. I wanted to get married and teach, so I turned it down. At 9:00 that night, Beth said to me, "I'm not ready to get married. I want to date my old boyfriend." I got in my car and drove to Iowa to see if I could get that assistantship. I got it, and we finished second in the country. Eventually, Beth and I got married. It's funny. People always say I have a love/hate relationship with my wife. I love her. She hates me. I think I persevered.

Perseverance is also important when it comes to playing with your kids. Sometimes they are going to be cranky. Sometimes they will complain so much you just want to give up. The important thing to remember is that, no matter what, it is all worth it.

Sometimes play can be challenging, but you will always remember those times. When I was a kid, I loved sports. I followed sports, too. I remember when Mr. Rodgers, a neighbor, took us to see the Pirates play the Cardinals. Everyone else ran over to the Pirates dugout before the game, but I went to the visitors' side. I was a huge Cardinals fan. When I got there, a few of the players were playing pepper. I was only 10 feet from them. Nippy Jones hit a foul into the stands. I got the ball and threw it back. All those guys signed that ball and gave it back to me.

Sometimes play can be challenging, but you will always remember those times.

The funny thing is, thinking about that ball reminds me of the challenges that come along with playing with your kids. My dad and I were outside playing baseball one day. He used that ball and threw me a submarine. It got past us and fell down into the sewer. I was disappointed, but I still remember it as a time my dad played with me.

It was such a different time then. My dad didn't play with us much. No dad did. We had family gatherings, a picnic four times a year, where we played pickup games. Other than that, I remember watching him play cards, poker and euchre.

Nowadays, when a father tells me he doesn't have time to play with his kids, I tell him he'll regret it. I have to ask parents what their priorities are. Sometimes the busiest parents are the best parents because they really focus on their kids when they get the chance to spend time with them.

> *Sometimes the busiest parents are the best parents because they really focus on their kids when they get the chance to spend time with them.*

I was busy when my kids were little. When I found the time, though, I did quality things with them. We always went to church as a family. We'd go to breakfast afterward. They would order everything they wanted. When I wanted to teach them how much it cost, I made it a game.

"Whoever guesses closest to the check wins a dollar," I said.

It was fun, and afterward they started questioning what things cost. We still play that game now when we go out.

There is nothing better than having fun with your kids. I will never forget all those moments of happiness.

No matter how fun it is to reminisce, it is important to remember one final thing. Let your kids have their life, and do not live vicariously through theirs. It is their life, and they need to live it.

It kind of reminds me of a joke I played on my daughter. Liz was getting ready to go to the prom. I ran upstairs and put my tuxedo on. When her date came to the door, I rushed down the stairs.

"I never went to the prom! This may be the only chance I have," I said.

Her date said, "No problem," but my daughter was mortified.

With my son looking to get into coaching, keeping neutral could have been even harder for me. For Skip, it was different. I took him around to look at schools. When he got to Notre Dame, he fell in love. He knew that's where he wanted to go. When I got hired there, he was already a student. One day, he made an appointment to see me. That was odd. When he showed up, he told me he wanted to be a coach.

"Talk to your mom first," I said. "But make sure she isn't armed."

SH: I remember going to see my dad when I decided I wanted to be a coach. We went out to dinner. I told him as soon as we sat down. He discouraged me. He did the same thing when I told him I wanted to go to Notre Dame. He has always been great about not giving me advice. He would never make my decision for me. Instead, he would ask me stuff like, "What do you think?" He would talk me through it, and I would end up answering my own question. So when I told him I wanted to be a coach, he told me I would have to move around a lot, that I would be in the office 12 hours a day, and that I would have to start as a lowly graduate assistant. But coaching has been great, and in the end I came to the decision on my own.

LH: Skip went into coaching for the right reasons, though. In fact, I didn't offer him a job. I wanted him to live his own life. But when Bobby Bowden offered him a position, I thought better of it and kept him on my staff.

LH: By today's standards, these stories might not sound so great. For the kids, though, this is the stuff they laugh about now. Times are obviously different, but there is a common theme. Your kids are only going to be kids once. Right now they are building the memories that they will return to again and again in their lives.

At the same time, parents have to make sure they keep living their own lives, as well. As a coach's family, we had to move around a lot. At one point, I thought about not taking a job because I thought it might be hard on the kids. I talked to my wife about it.

"When they are 21, they can live wherever they want. We can't live their lives," she said. "And they can't live ours."

When it comes right down to it, that is the biggest challenge as a parent. You cannot do it for them. You are responsible to keep them safe and teach them what is right and wrong in life. Sometimes you have to let them make mistakes. They have to live their own life.

SH: Everyone asks me what I learned from my father, whether as a dad or as a coach. I think it is about attitude. My dad used to say that you spell love, "t-i-m-e." So if you bring work home with you, that time you have with your kids is not going to be great. Instead, have a positive attitude. Leave your troubles at the door. If you are not willing to spend quality time with your kids, there are millions of advertisers out there willing to do it for you.

LH: When you see your kid sitting on a couch or playing a video game, this is the challenge, and it is your responsibility. Get them up, play with them, and be active. All it takes is a little pep talk.

Herm Edwards | Play to Win the Game

Herm Edwards is an NFL analyst for ESPN. He played professional football for 10 seasons with the Philadelphia Eagles, Los Angeles Rams, and Atlanta Falcons. He was the head coach of the New York Jets and Kansas City Chiefs. His play against the New York Giants, in which he ran a fumble back for a touchdown to win the game in the final seconds, caused teams to start "taking a knee" to run out the clock. He is the father of a son and two daughters.

I first said it when I was coaching the Jets: "You play to win the game." I already knew it was the greatest thing about sports. You know what? It applies to life, too.

In athletics, most people look at the scoreboard to determine who wins and who loses. I think you have to go a little bit beyond that. You have to look at yourself in the mirror to see if you put forth your best effort. Never is that more true than when you are a parent. It is easy to get caught up in life and lose sight of the importance of being a parent.

Herm Edwards with his wife and daughters

Trust me, it is a lot harder being a parent and watching your kids struggle through life than it is being a coach. You want them to do well. In sports, you want them to catch every pass, and every tackle is important. In life, you want them to make the right choices and go down the right paths. When things are good, you sit back and watch. You feel proud.

My main focus as a parent is to create an environment where my children are loved, nurtured, and taught the lessons of life. Through sports, you can teach young people a lot about life. Life mirrors athletics. However, in athletics, "life" happens in a time span of approximately three hours. You have your ups, your downs. You have to make decisions in thirty seconds. You have to deal with the highs of making a good play and the other emotions when a play doesn't go well. How you control your actions is critical.

Those things happen to you off the field, too. There are certain things you can't control. The only thing you really can control is your emotions. All you can do is prepare yourself to play the best you can.

When you are young, you don't know much about what your parents want. You are just playing for the joy of play. Eventually, you learn the importance of competing against yourself. I remember talking to my son while he was growing up. I said, "It's not about the opponent. It's really about yourself." When you get caught up in your opponent, your play will vary. When you face a great opponent, you are going to get up for the game. If you are playing a lesser opponent, you go in thinking you don't have to put in as much effort to win. And that's when you lose the true meaning of competition. It is really about what you have to do to get better—to win the game.

As parents, we all try to provide for our children. We all want to give them more than our parents were able to give us. No matter what our position is in life, though, there are two things that we have to pass on.

First, you give your children your name. They can't choose who their parents are. They are who they are from the start. What is up to them is how they are going to carry that on. What is their legacy going to be?

The second thing is that you give them wisdom. You let them know when they are traveling down the wrong road. You say, "I've traveled that road. You don't need to go down that one." Whether they choose to go down it or not, you've given them the wisdom to make the best decision they can. Parents can give their kids those two things, regardless of where they came from, where they work, or what race they are.

> *No matter what our position is in life, though, there are two things that we have to pass on. First, you give your children your name. The second thing is that you give them wisdom.*

The first part is easy. Your name is more about how you live your life. No matter what, your kids are going to watch you. They are going to see everything you do, and they are going to learn from it all—the good and the bad.

The second part, giving your kids the wisdom they need to make good decisions, is harder. It takes time. The best way to spend that time, and the way in which kids learn the best, is play.

When you say that parents should play more with their kids, the first thing you usually hear is, "How do we find the time?" Sometimes you just make time, no matter how busy you are. For me, it was the spring. I went to all my son's spring football practices. My wife and I would bring the lounge chairs and sit in the sun. It got funny when the college recruiters came around. They'd approach me and introduce themselves. I'd laugh and say, "You know, you have to convince my wife, not me."

When I was young, my father was in the service, so he was gone a lot. Early on, I grew up on an Army base. Then we moved to Seaside, California. I didn't play Pop Warner. My mom didn't want me to play football. The only sports I played from the time I was about eight to around 12 years old was at the park with my buddies on Saturdays. In elementary school, we had recess and played kickball, volleyball, and touch football. I didn't start organized sports until junior high. I went out for all the teams, but I didn't play tackle football until high school.

The one thing I did do growing up was play against kids who were older than I was. I was big for my age. In basketball I'd go up against guys two or three years older and get beaten down. It was a way of life in our neighborhood.

Unlike parents today, mine were not involved in my athletic career. My father was gone, and my mother worked all the time. Plus, she was scared of athletics. In fact, in my first year of high school, the coach had to come to my house and convince her to let me play football.

In my senior year, my mom and dad came to one of my basketball games. It was the first game that they came to watch. It was the first time my mom had ever seen me play a sport. She was German and she knew about sports, but she didn't understand how important they were in the U.S. She had no idea about scholarships. My parents were busy working and trying to provide for me and my sister. I kept telling them I was going to play sports in college. Even when coaches started coming to the house, my mom said, "Why are they coming here?"

Seeing my parents in the stands that day, it was a thrill. Having my mom and dad watch me play was one of the highlights of my life. The funny thing is, my dad never came to one of my football games until I was playing at the

University of California. Mom wouldn't see me play again until I was with the Philadelphia Eagles.

Some of the guys my dad worked with were Cal alums. They told him I was playing pretty well. They told him he needed to take Saturday off and have a look. So they took him up. It was the Washington State game. I had four interceptions. I ran the second one back for a touchdown. I have no doubt that his being there was the reason I played so well.

The next time he saw me play, it was against the Rams in Los Angeles. It was the game during which I got my first interception as a professional. It was off Joe Namath. I was so excited my dad was there. In both cases, my father just being there in the stands helped me play two of the best games of my career. That is the kind of effect parents have on kids. As parents it is easy to forget that.

When my son, Marcus, was little, it was tough for me to be around as much as I wanted to. I was with the Philadelphia Eagles at the time. I would make it home to watch him play basketball, but football season was tough. When I retired, he came to Tampa. I was working as a coach with Tony Dungy, and he was great. He gave us time off to be with our families. I got to most of Marcus's high school games. But when he got to college I was coaching the Jets, so things got tough again.

The one thing I learned through all this is that I didn't want to coach my kids. I just wanted to be a parent. I would say, "Son, if you want help, I will give you help. But you have to ask. Don't come home crying about your coach. Listen to him." I never sat in the stands and questioned Marcus's coaches. I didn't want to put the man in that kind of situation. He knew I was a coach. I wanted it to be about Marcus, not me.

Sometimes making the time isn't enough. Sometimes you have to make bigger choices so that you don't miss out on your kids' childhood. In raising my daughters, I have decided that to continue coaching would be unfair to them. I look at my girls and say to myself, "I want to watch them grow up." I want to make time for them. Sometimes you have to change what you do to make sure they get what they need.

You can't, however, change who you are, and that was hard on Marcus sometimes. I remember being in Tampa when Marcus played football on Friday nights. Several players from the Tampa Bay Buccaneers would be there in the stands to watch him play. John Lynch, the Pro Bowl safety and Marcus' godfather, would also be sitting in the audience. I remember Keyshawn Johnson, the great Jets and Buccaneers wide receiver, up in the stands yelling, "Throw No. 9 the ball!" That's the pressure my son already felt—without me even being his coach.

I never coached him, but I did let him be around professional players. I wanted him to see what football was really all about, not just what he saw on television. I wanted him to see the hard work that went on behind the scenes. I wanted him to know it wasn't going to be easy, and sometimes it wasn't even going to be fun. I would let him play seven-on-seven and one-on-one with the Bucs. Before that, I let him be the ball boy.

I tried to teach him, and now my girls, two things. First, enjoy the game. Second, be a good sport. I'll give you a quick story about my son.

I wanted my son to see what football was really all about, not just what he saw on television. I wanted him to see the hard work that went on behind the scenes. I wanted him to know it wasn't going to be easy, and sometimes it wasn't even going to be fun.

It was the third game of his senior year. He was a good player on a good team. When he came out for warm-ups, he had his gloves around his face mask. Maybe he learned that from Randy Moss when he watched him on television. When we saw Marcus, my wife looked at me. She said, "No." And I said, "Oh, yeah."

I quietly walked down the stands and out on the field. I motioned to Marcus and said, "Come here for a minute." When Marcus walked over, I said, "Let me tell you something, partner. See those gloves around your face mask? You have a choice right now. Get those gloves from around your face mask, or you are done playing football." He took them off and never put his gloves around his face mask again.

It was a great teaching opportunity for me. We don't do things like that. We don't disrespect the uniform. We do not disrespect football. Not that way. You are going to do it the right way.

Sometimes the only way your kids can learn is by living through the tough times. You have to let them make choices. They need to learn that there are consequences to those choices. If you choose to play video games over doing your homework, I am going to take the game away for a week. That helps them grow.

There are other challenges to being active with your kids. For kids today, play has changed. It is definitely more organized now than it was when I was growing up, especially for young girls. In the 1960s, girls who played sports were considered tomboys. There were a couple of girls who played with us, and they were tough. They could hold their own. Today, girls can do everything boys do, including sports.

> *For kids today, play has changed.*

The thing about sports—what is great about it—is that everyone is competing. It is not about how much money your family has or what race you are. Religion doesn't matter. It's just about athletics. It is a great melting pot. On top of that, it is about being part of a team. It is not so much about yourself but about the team.

Playing sports has its benefits. Not only are you giving your kids the wisdom they need, but you are keeping them healthy. I am a 4:30 AM guy. I get up in the morning and put in two hours of exercise six days a week. I run, lift, and get on the machines. It is part of my makeup. I enjoy it. It sets up my day. And I like getting up early like that because it's "my time." Then all of my exercise is done, and I feel good going to work.

Physical fitness should be like brushing your teeth. You have to do it. But you know what? You are doing it for you. So be a little selfish. When you feel good about yourself, you look at life a little differently. Exercise provides energy. It is a great release. You should look forward to it.

> *Physical fitness should be like brushing your teeth. You have to do it. But you know what? You are doing it for you. So be a little selfish. When you feel good about yourself, you look at life a little differently.*

For kids today, the level of physical fitness has declined. When I was young, there was the Presidential Physical Fitness test. You had to take gym. Every kid had to put on shorts and do certain things. We've gotten away from that.

I think it has tarnished kids' abilities to go outside and play athletics. They play it on machines now. Video games are almost used as babysitters now. Kids will sit in a room for three hours. The games are very competitive, but the kids aren't doing it. They are not active. They are pressing a button, not running and jumping and catching.

When I grew up, you had to play. Video games were not readily available. Even if they were, I would not have wanted to play them all day. I would have wanted to play. In my day, you were going to play a sport every season of the year. It was mandatory. You were just going to do it.

I hear some parents saying they can't control how much their kids play video games. I think they can. For Marcus, I remember he could only play half an hour a day. Then he was going outside, no excuses. If it was cold, I told him to put on a jacket and some gloves.

You can't just let them decide. When I was young, my dad had us doing chores. We cut the grass and raked the yard. That wasn't necessarily what I wanted to do, but I did it. Parents have to see physical activity the same way. Maybe your kids see it as a chore. So what? They need to be active, and if they get outside as much as we used to, they'll grow to love it.

All of this sounds like a lot. Your kids are growing up fast. You might think it is too late to make a difference. That's not true. Go back to what every coach probably said to you when you were growing up: "The game isn't over until the whistle blows." I was fortunate enough to be part of something that illustrates that more than anything else.

> *Your kids are growing up fast. You might think it is too late to make a difference. That's not true. Go back to what every coach probably said to you when you were growing up: "The game isn't over until the whistle blows."*

Some people call it "the Miracle at the Meadowlands," but New York Giants fans call it "the Fumble." It happened at Giants Stadium in 1978. I was with the Eagles, and we were losing to the Giants 17–12. It was in the final seconds of the game. The Giants could have taken a knee and won the game, but no one did that back then. In fact, that play came into being because of this one.

What happened was that Giants quarterback Joe Pisarcik took the snap and tried to hand it to fullback Larry Csonka.

They botched the handoff. I picked up the fumble and ran it for a touchdown, winning what seemed like an unwinnable game for the Eagles.

Except for the final gun, that game was over. Then the ball was on the ground. But the fumble alone didn't decide the winner. If I was not doing my job getting across the line of scrimmage, I would not have been involved in the play. There still had to be a botched snap. There still had to be a fumble. But I had to do my job beforehand to be in a position to score.

A lot of things had to go wrong for the "Miracle" to happen. But a lot of things had to go right, too. It is no different with kids. You have to be there, doing your job, if you want to be in a position to win the game. Even if your kid is in high school, the whistle hasn't blown. You never know.

My dad worked his entire life. In addition to being in the military, he worked weekends doing yard work. I would go with him to earn a little extra cash. He handed me a broom once and said, "See this? Don't ever be afraid of it." He was talking about hard work.

When I was very young, he told me we didn't have a lot of money. He said, "I can't get you a new car, but I am going to give you two things that you will have for the rest of your life. I am going to give you a good last name, and I am going to give you wisdom."

That conversation came to mind when I was talking to Marcus about the gloves in his face mask. It shaped me as a dad. See, parents teach their kids no matter what. It can be good or bad. Either way, it affects our kids. I think it is time we see that and do something about how kids are today. They need to be active. To do that, we need to share some of that wisdom with them. We need to let them know that sometimes video games and sitting on the couch aren't the right paths. We need to share with them the wisdom of hard work and physical fitness. It isn't always easy. Sometimes it means we need to get up off the couch, too. But I guarantee that if we do, our kids will make the most of that name we gave them.

It is all too easy to forget what life's real game is all about. Sports are great, and they are definitely part of it, but the real game is being the best parent you can be. There's really nothing more to it than that. You give your kids your name, and you give them the wisdom you've spent a lifetime learning. Then you do your best to coach them through the hard times and celebrate their successes. No matter what, it comes down to one thing. You have to play to win that game. Your kids depend on it.

Laila Ali | Building a Relationship

Laila Ali is a professional boxer. Her father, Muhammad Ali, is a legend. Laila was the second daughter of Ali and Veronica Porsche. She is married to former professional football player Curtis Conway. She has one son, Curtis Muhammad Conway Jr.

My dad was very sweet. He kissed us all the time, and he was not a disciplinarian. He would come into the dining room when my sister and I were eating dinner. If we said we didn't like our vegetables, he would come up and grab them off our plates. Maybe he would eat them; maybe he would put them in the potted plant sitting in the corner of the room. There was proof. The dining room often had the odor of rotting vegetables.

Dad was a joker. He liked to put on these crazy masks, scary masks. Sometimes it would be a goblin or Dracula, crazy stuff like that, and he would jump out and scare us. One of my fondest memories of the time I spent with him was when he would show up with his brown Rolls-Royce.

Muhammad Ali with daughters Laila (right) and Hana

I have eight brothers and sisters but not all from the same mother. We would all be together, and we would climb in. My father would put the top down and drive us on Wilshire Boulevard. We might go to a place like Bob's Big Boy—you know, a neighborhood diner. On the way, he might pull over and give a homeless man a $100 bill.

He loved a crowd. People would wave and shout, "There's Ali!" He would stand there and do magic tricks for everyone. As I got older, I realized how great a man my father was. He treated people with kindness no matter what their station was in life. He is still an inspiration today. It is crazy. He brings out so much emotion in people. They are not just looking for his autograph; it is something more than that. He stood for something bigger than just the sport. That's just who he is as a man.

Now that I am a mom, I have a whole new perspective on parenthood. I know how important it is to build a relationship with your kids. Ignoring them or yelling at them doesn't work. Without that relationship, your kids will not trust you. Just telling them what is right and wrong is not enough. It takes a loving, open relationship to get your kids to talk to you about things that are up in their life.

Kids want structure in their life, but parenting can be one of the hardest jobs in the world. People should take pride in being good parents. I do, and I believe in educating myself on being an even better parent. I might look in a book or ask someone I respect for advice. It takes planning. You have to sit down and think about how you are going to raise your kids.

Parenting can be one of the hardest jobs in the world.

Now I am raising my son. He is 18 months old. He is a lean, mean muscle machine already. My husband says he is fast. He'll tell little Curtis to get ready, and Curtis gets into a football stance. I don't really want him to play football like his dad or box like me. If it has to be one or the other, I'd rather he'd play football. No one, especially not a boxer, wants her kid to box. My dad did not want me to box. It is a dangerous sport, and he didn't think women should do it. He supported me, but he didn't necessarily like it. In the end, the passion came from his blood. There was nothing either of us could do about it.

As for my son, I think he will play sports, though. He has that tenacity already. He does not give up. If you are wrestling with him and get him good, he'll come back and get you. I love to get down and play with him. He has learning games, and I read to him all the time. He loves to be rough and tumble and play hide and seek. We go to the park for walks. He is also a sweet little kid, I think because he sees me and my husband kissing and hugging.

For me, my son comes first. Everyone who knows me knows that. I don't know if that is the way it is with most parents. They are caught up in work and everything else that is going on in their lives. Kids should come before anything else.

I look at my son and I think about my father. He knew how to treat people, and I want my son to be the same way. I want him to learn that it is not okay to step on someone to get ahead. I want him to learn respect and dignity. I also want him to be himself. I see people who act one way when they are around people who are more powerful than they are, then pump their chest out when they are around someone they think has less power. I want my son to be nice to people. Making fun of others is a form of insecurity. I want him to be sensitive toward others, and I want him to take that out into society. My father taught me all of that, and in turn I will teach my son.

I know it is not always going to be easy. I already worry about sending my son out into the world. I know it is part of life. We all went through it. I also know that I cannot stand in his way.

Laila and Muhammad Ali

At the same time, I look forward to him growing up and us having a great relationship. I look forward to him becoming a great man and watching him put the things I teach him into effect. It is amazing to think that I created this human being. I worry that not everyone sees it that way. They don't plan ahead, and they just take it day by day. They way I see it is that in life, if I want something, if I have a passion, I plan for success and I practice at it. I think everyone should feel the same way.

I take my son to see his grandfather. Dad is funny because of his illness. He likes to play with his cards and dominos. In the morning, he sits on his bed and eats fruit and watches the news. That is the best time to visit him, before he takes his medications. One time, my son crawled up there and tried to get some of dad's fruit and play with his dominos. Dad scooped them all up and pulled away. Laughing, I thought he had really gotten stingy in his old age.

My son looks a lot like his grandfather. I often think about what lesson I learned from my father that I use the most as a parent. My father was very busy. He was gone a lot of the time. I have learned that is not how I want it to be for my son. At the same time, I would never dream of changing my dad. He is a great man, and he made a difference in so many lives. I would not trade what he means to the world.

For my son it will be different. I want to be there for him. I do not want to miss anything. I don't want my child to be raised by a nanny like I was. They come and go, and you can never really know their values and morals or how they are treating your child.

So many kids are growing up like that. Parents want the nanny to get their child good and tired so they go to sleep once they get home from work. I don't understand why they chose to have children in the first place. On the other side of the spectrum, there are people out there having sex irresponsibly. They are on welfare and having children. Maybe they don't see that when their kids get older, there is going to be a problem.

I know life gets in the way. I know that people need to work, but you have to stop and take that time. When I have a bad day and I have a lot going on, I see my son smiling and it changes my day. Sometimes I might be on the computer and he comes and tugs on my leg. I stop and give him my attention. It drives me crazy thinking about the fact that not everyone is doing that. I think that is why our society is the way it is. People today don't think about the world as a whole. Everyone is out for themselves. They do not see how we are all connected. All the robbing, bullying, killing, shootings—it all comes from the fact that we as a people are not concerned with others' feelings.

I think as parents we need to educate ourselves, especially if you don't know how to raise a child. There are so many books out there that can help. Maybe they can inspire people. Parenting is a hard job, especially if you do it right. It needs to be taught, and you have to love yourself before you can learn. You have to teach your kids that what they do affects other people.

> *I know life gets in the way. I know that people need to work, but you have to stop and take that time. When I have a bad day and I have a lot going on, I see my son smiling and it changes my day.*

In the end, I think we should all just keep it simple. We should cherish each day and spend as much time as we can together. Enjoy your kids. You'll be thankful when you get older and you have children who still want to be there for you.

Jim and Joseph Kelly | Appreciate Every Moment

Jim Kelly is a former NFL and USFL quarterback. He led the Buffalo Bills to four consecutive Super Bowls and was inducted into the Pro Football Hall of Fame. His son, Hunter, passed away from Krabbe disease at age eight. He has two daughters.

Joseph Kelly is the father of Jim Kelly. A retired machinist, he was raised in an orphanage in Pittsburgh. He is the father of six boys.

Father and son talked to us about the values that cemented their perspectives on parenting and the unyielding power of love in the face of hardship.

Jim Kelly: My father is a man full of quotations. His words have guided me through my life. Sometimes I didn't follow them word for word, but I always listened.

"Appreciate everything you have and enjoy life because you only live once," he told me. As a kid, I never dreamed how much that would ring true. When my wife got pregnant with our first child I quickly learned the hard truth of those words.

Before my son was born, I remember dreaming about everything I would do with him as he grew up. I pictured teaching him to throw a football and to hunt. I imagined days spent outside, his little legs moving quickly as he chased me around the yard. I took those things as a given. Those are the kinds of things my dad did with me. Of course I would do them with my son.

Right after I retired from football, Hunter was born. It was Valentine's Day, which is my birthday, too. He looked so healthy that I still had no indication of what would happen next. I still thought everything was fine and that I would raise him like my father raised me and all my brothers. After a few months, my father's words came back to me. We knew Hunter wasn't feeling well, but when he was diagnosed with Krabbe disease and given 15 months to live, I knew our lives would never be the same again.

My dad's advice helped me to cherish every day I had with Hunter.

My dad's advice helped me to cherish every day I had with Hunter. He was a light to us all. And he taught us the true meaning of courage and strength. I watched him struggle every day. He beat the doctor's sentence—Hunter fought for eight and a half years.

From Hunter, I learned a simple lesson. Never take things for granted. I remember that on the day he was born, I thanked God he was healthy. Then I watched what he went through after he got sick. It tore me apart. And

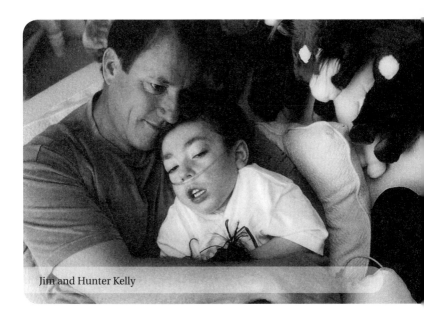
Jim and Hunter Kelly

it made me realize that some of the smaller things that I thought were bad were not really that bad. I watched that little boy fight his whole life.

Joseph Kelly: Jim was so close to Hunter. He took it really bad. I thought it was going to change everything. We tried to console him. I'd tell him that it must be the way God wants it to be, that Hunter was looking down on him and taking care of his family. It's hard. I can understand. His only boy taken away before he could teach him football or take him fishing.

Jim: There are moments with Hunter that I'll never forget. Some of them were just simple things, times we spent

> *Hunter made me a better dad. He taught me just how precious every day is. If there is any advice I could give fathers out there, it would be: Play with your kids every day. You have no idea what the future might bring.*

together. I remember one time when he was with me and the Bills weren't doing so well. We were watching the game together and I'd say, "Hunter, enough of this game." I'd go into the video archives and take out some of Daddy's games. He would light up and get excited. It was pretty cool.

I miss Hunter every day. I pray to him every day and remember the lessons I was fortunate enough to learn from his short life with us. Hunter made me a better dad. He taught me just how precious every day is. If there is any advice I could give fathers out there, it would be to play with your kids every day. You have no idea what the future might bring.

Jim: I came from a family of six boys. My father was raised in an orphanage in Pennsylvania. He was a baby when he was first taken there, and he never knew his parents. He lived there his entire childhood.

My dad didn't talk about that time much, but he was proud of where he came from. He didn't have a family of his own growing up, but you'd never know it. Looking at our family now and how close we are, you'd think he had a great role model who helped him become the father he was. Somehow he figured it out for himself.

When he left the orphanage and headed out on his own, he eventually met my mom. He was in the Navy at the time, and they decided to start a family. Their first child was a son; then came three more. My dad was pretty happy at that point, but my mom wanted a girl. She talked him into one more try.

She had twin boys next. My mom never got her girl. We liked to joke with her that it must have been like a stab to her heart. She didn't want another boy, let alone two. My mom had a favorite saying: "I wouldn't sell my kids for any amount of money in the world, but there were some days I would have gladly given them away."

As parents, we can all laugh at that statement. But for my folks, it might have been true. My dad had six hungry boys to feed, and it wasn't always easy. He had to work three jobs sometimes. Coming from the orphanage, he knew the meaning of hard work, and he made a point of teaching us that by example.

Joseph: When I first met my wife, we talked about it. We wanted a close family. I never expected six boys. They're all still close. At Christmas we get together. I like to see all my grandkids—I have 15.

February 14, Valentine's Day, the birthday my son and I share, is the perfect day for us to remember Hunter. Every year, our foundation, Hunter's Hope, holds an event at the Ralph Wilson Stadium Field House: Hunter's Day of Hope for Children. We urge people to bring their kids along, to help parents realize how important that day is and realize how important their kids are. Now we get about 5,000 people at the event.

Coming from the orphanage, my father knew the meaning of hard work and he made a point of teaching us that by example.

Jim: Dad learned other things from the orphanage too. For Christmas one year he gave us all a pair of boxing gloves. He said he was tired of all of our fighting. So when we got into it, he told us to go out to the garage and put on a football helmet and the gloves. Then we'd have at it.

Believe me, those gloves got mangled pretty quickly. My dad would tape them up, which made them even heavier. I learned that boxing is a great workout, especially for me. See, my younger brothers were twins. So if I got into an argument and got sent to the garage with one of them, the other one always came, too. I ended up with twice the workout. One thing I know, it made us tough. A quality I've been thankful for so many times since.

Joseph: Well, I'll tell you. When I was a boy in the orphanage, the nuns didn't put up with us kids fighting. They'd take us to the gym and give us boxing gloves. They'd say, "You two fight it out." And the nuns would stand there and watch. So with my boys, I figured if the nuns did it, it must be good. I'd give them the gloves and say, "Whoever opens the door wins." I'd close the door when I left, but stay and look through the window to make sure no one got hurt. It was always more dancing than fighting.

Jim: That wasn't the only thing my dad taught us. Even with all his jobs, he always made the time to play with us.

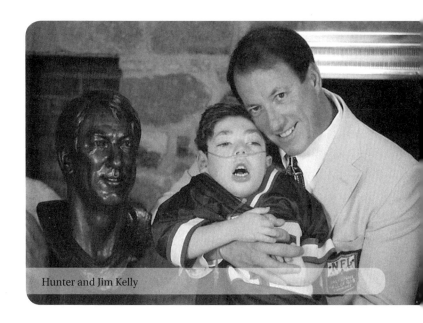

Hunter and Jim Kelly

I'm sure it wasn't easy to find the energy to do that with six growing boys, but he did.

His jobs weren't the only obstacles he had to overcome when it came to playing with us. My dad didn't learn how to play sports as a boy. The orphanage didn't have them. That didn't stop him, though. He read up on how to play football and baseball. He even coached our Little League teams.

Every day my dad had time, he was teaching us sports. He pushed us playing football, baseball, and basketball. He was at every game. I don't think he missed a single one.

I laugh when I think back to how much importance my dad placed on physical activity. Growing up, my school was only about 100 yards from our house. I walked home every day for lunch. My dad, when he was on the night shift, would be home waiting for me, my lunch already made. I couldn't eat it, though—not right away. First, he'd have me out back practicing football. No practice, no lunch. He meant it, too.

Joseph: Sometimes Jim was hard to deal with. I'd tell him if he practiced hard enough he'd be exceptional. I pounded that into his head. I don't know if he listened, but apparently he did. I was on shift work and home at noon. I used to make him practice football before I'd feed him. He'd sneak away to his buddies' and probably eat there, then go back to school. In the evening, I'd catch him and have him practice. I'd say, "No eating until you practice," but my wife would overrule that. That's usually the way it is, isn't it?

Jim: Like I said, he is a man full of quotations. One of his favorites was: "Just remember one thing—you'll never get anywhere if you don't work at it." He knew that if I wanted to be great and wanted my dreams to come true, I couldn't sit back and watch. He told me that nothing would be given to me for free and that I had to earn it. He instilled that mentality in all his boys by getting out there and playing with us and by showing us what hard work was and what it meant to our future.

Don't get me wrong, I didn't always like it. Growing up, especially when I was younger, I definitely got tired of him telling me to go out and play all the time. But after a point, he didn't have to tell me anymore. The funny thing is that I started to enjoy it, partially because he was out there with me a lot of the time. It wasn't him just telling me to do something. He was a consistent force.

Joseph: I worked three shifts and a couple of odd jobs to put food on the table. But I found time to play with my boys. I'd run patterns or snap the ball, whatever I could do. I didn't even start playing golf until after I retired. I didn't have time for golf. I wanted to spend time watching my kids play basketball and baseball and football.

Jim: Throughout my life, Dad's the one who stuck with me through thick and thin. I remember days when I would have to run lap after lap just to stay under weight for football as a kid. I wasn't fat, but I was the tallest kid, which is good for being a quarterback but bad for trying to make weight for the championship game. My dad was always there for me, waiting for me at the end and encouraging me, telling me that all the pain was worth it.

When I signed with the Bills, I remember the one thing my dad asked me for in return for all the time and love he gave—it was a mobile home. He wanted it so he could load up all his buddies from East Brady, Pennsylvania, and come tailgate and watch my games. He wanted to share everything his sons did with all his friends.

> *Growing up, especially when I was younger, I definitely got tired of him telling me to go out and play all the time. But after a point, he didn't have to tell me anymore. The funny thing is that I started to enjoy it, partially because he was out there with me a lot of the time.*

My dad is 80 years old now and has had three stents and had a heart attack last year. But he still plays golf and works out. He's one of the guys, and I cherish every day we have together.

⚜

Jim: Now, I'm the dad. I have two daughters I worship. And I've been fortunate enough to realize how important our time is together. My dad showed me how much playing and spending time together means, and my son showed me how fragile life can be. So I try to spend as much time with my daughters as I can. I coach them in basketball and softball. I play in the yard with them. I do everything I can to teach them the importance of physical activity and the fun you can have playing as a family.

My kids are just great. I played ball with them from the time they were about one month old. I remember two years ago I coached my daughter's championship basketball game. She was in the sixth grade. We were undefeated, and so was the other team. "The Star Spangled Banner" started, and I didn't notice anything at first. I was focusing on getting ready for the game. But then I realized it sounded familiar. It was Whitney Houston. And I realized it was a recording from Super Bowl XXV. All of a sudden in my mind I saw Scott Norwood's kick going wide right.

And history repeated itself at the end of my daughter's game. It was 20–19 and our best shooter was on the line. There was no time left. She put up her foul shot, and I

The Kelly family

watched it go wide right. After the game I told my daughter about it and she groaned.

"Wide right again."

If I hadn't coached her team, I wouldn't have been part of that moment. I thank God I was. I'll never forget it.

I love watching them grow up. Just like my dad, I know there are times when I drive them nuts. When they fall down and it's a bad one, I take care of them and hug them. But when it isn't, I've been known to say, "Shake it off, you'll be all right."

They say, "Daddy, you always say that."

And my wife says, "Jimmy, you've got to understand you have daughters."

But I laugh, think about my dad, and say, "My girls are going to be tough."

I know how important that lesson is. It isn't always going to be easy for them. Bad things are going to happen. When they do, they need to be ready, and they need to have the strength to pull themselves back up. It's a lesson my dad taught me through our time playing together. It's a lesson that helped get me through the loss of my son. And it is a lesson I am teaching my girls now through our time together.

Joseph: When I talk to the boys on the phone, I say, "I love you, son," and they say, "I love you, Dad," before hanging up. When we see each other, we hug each other. They give me a little kiss on the cheek. It means a lot to me. They do it with their kids, too. That means a lot.

Jim: As I finish this up, it's funny—I find myself thinking about one of my mom's quotes, not one of my dad's. She wished she had a girl, but she wouldn't trade her sons for any amount of money. I think about Hunter and the stuff we might have done. If I had the opportunity, I might give some moments of my life away, some of the struggles and the pain, but I wouldn't sell my life for any amount of money in the world. I'll never take it for granted and, like my dad said and my son taught me firsthand, I try to appreciate every moment with my girls like it's our last together.

Joseph: Jim really loved his mom. I often saw him grab her by the hand. He'd put his fingers between hers. She thought that was the greatest thing. Now I see him do that same thing with his daughters. Jim loves his girls. He gets involved in the girls' sports, softball and swimming. You couldn't ask for a better dad. It warms my heart when I see him with his children.

Jim: I hope someday my kids look back and think about the time they spent with their dad. Maybe they'll remember some quote I said. If they do, I hope it's this:

"Play every day—appreciate every moment."

.

Tony and Eduardo Pérez | Leaving Home

Tony Pérez was the first Cuban to be named to the Major League Baseball Hall of Fame. He was part of the "Big Red Machine," the Cincinnati Reds in the 70s. He won back-to-back World Series in 1975 and 1976. He was a seven-time All-Star. He has two sons, Eduardo and Victor.

Eduardo Pérez made it to the majors after playing for Florida State University. He played for the California Angels, Cincinnati Reds, St. Louis Cardinals, Tampa Bay Devil Rays, Cleveland Indians, and Seattle Mariners. He and his wife are raising their two daughters in Puerto Rico, where he manages winter league. He is also an analyst for ESPN's Baseball Tonight.

C*iego de Ávila is a province in the center of the island of Cuba. It is best known for its two cays, Cayo Coco and Cayo Guillermo. They have become a popular resort destinations due to their sparkling white sand beaches and the Caribbean's biggest reef. Otherwise, most of the province is predominantly covered with farmland for sugar cane and* *fruit trees. The province is speckled with small towns, one of which is Central de Violeta.*

Tony Pérez: I was raised in Central de Violeta, Cuba. There were not too many big cities around, only small towns. About 3,000 people lived in my town. Most of them worked for the sugar cane company. We worked and played baseball. That's about it.

I was raised way down in the country. We had chickens and pigs in the backyard. Over there, no one had much money. So we would get a small pig and feed it for a year. We could get it up to three or four hundred pounds. Then we sacrificed it to get the meat. We used every bit.

Once my brother raised a chicken. It was given to him as a chick. My brother was in love with it. He named it, and it grew up in the backyard. It got to be so big and beautiful that one day I told my other brother, "Hey, that chicken is going to get too old." Old chicken is no good. It gets tough.

Without him knowing, we killed that chicken and cooked it up. My brother ate it along with us. He said, "Nice chicken." After the meal he was looking around for his chicken, and we told him he had just eaten it. He was heartbroken.

Even from a young age, I saw how hard my father worked. I was number five of six children. I had two brothers and three sisters. It was hard to raise all of us, to give us something to eat and send us to school. It was difficult, but we were a happy family. We were together. They were happy days for me. I was raised in a good family with a lot of love.

My father worked at the sugar cane company. He had to be to work at 3:00 AM, so he was up at 2:30 AM. He got off at 11:00 AM. From there, he worked part time as a painter. He worked all day and went to bed about 7:00 PM. All he did was work.

I remember those days. I would go to school Monday through Friday, but the whole time I could not wait for the weekend. That is when we played baseball. That is all we did. I would play with my brother and the other kids. It was nothing special. We would play wherever we could. There were not too many cars in the town, so often we just played in the street.

Unfortunately, I didn't have much time to play with my dad. He worked all the time. But I remember we used to listen to games on the radio together. We didn't live close to Havana; it was about 11 hours away. During winter league baseball, we could tune in to games maybe once a week. The games started at 9:00 PM. We would just sit there and listen until midnight.

There were four teams playing back then, and each of us had our favorites. My three sisters liked the same team my father did, the Havanas. My older brother and I liked the Fuegos. We would talk about the players and the game. It was a great time.

When I got older, I got very good at baseball. At the same time, I went to work in the sugar cane company with my father. I would get up with him at 2:30, and we would walk together to the factory. I didn't have to be there the whole day, but often I would not leave until 11:00, staying there to help my father. Our job was printing the name of the company on the sacks for the sugar. Sometimes the printer took longer, but we had to reach our quota.

I started working there when I was 15 years old, although I was not supposed to until I was 16. If I had stayed in Cuba, that is where I would have spent my life—in that sugar factory. Baseball had a different plan for me.

Revolution

The late 1950s and early 1960s were a turbulent time in the history of Cuba. After a decade of declining economic stability, the island, consisting of a large middle class, suffered an increase in unemployment and a growing public dissatisfaction with the government.

In 1956 Fidel Castro returned to the island from Mexico. He brought with him a group of dissidents whose goal was to start a revolution. By 1958 he led an insurgency out of the mountains, and they captured Santa Clara. The leader of Cuba at the time, Batista, fled the country, passing leadership to Fidel Castro, his brother Raul, and Che Guevara. Their forces entered the capital in 1959.

TP: One of the most important lessons I learned from my father was discipline. When I worked with him, he stressed that we had to be there on time. It was not always easy for me to get up at 2:30 AM. Sometimes I would go out late to the movies, coming back at 11:00 PM. I barely got to sleep and I would have to be up again and on the way to work.

That experience taught me discipline. I learned to be on time, and when I came to America to play ball, that is something that the managers asked of me. They would say, "If you are going to be late, call. But I want everyone here on time." That is a big reason I was able to open the door to a Major League career.

One of the most important lessons I learned from my father was discipline. When I worked with him, he stressed that we had to be there on time.

In 1960 I left Cuba for the first time. I was 17 when the Cincinnati Reds signed me. I did not get a signing bonus—only a plane ticket and an exit visa. I got on a plane and left my home and my family behind. I ended up in Geneva, New York, and started playing in the minor leagues. I can still remember how cold it was. I could feel it in my bones. It reminded me just how much I missed my family and my home—and the discipline taught by my father.

When the opportunity arose for me to leave Cuba to play ball, my father told me to go. He said to me, "There is nothing down here for you. I have been working my whole life in Cuba, and we have nothing. Go and get a good future. If you can help us out, help us out. If you have the chance to come back, come back." My mother did not want me to go. She was afraid that she would never see me again. It must have been awful for her.

At first, I was able to come back. After that first year, 1960, I visited during the off-season. In 1961 I returned too, and everything was still fine. In 1962 I broke my leg in the minors and came back to Cuba. By the time I was ready to return again in 1963, everything became complicated. The relationship between the United States and Cuba had become more strained. I missed all of spring training that year because I could not leave Cuba until May.

That was when my father said I should not come back. He was afraid the communists would never let me leave again. So I flew out in 1963 and didn't return for 10 years.

The Big Leagues

Eduardo Pérez: My father taught me a lesson that helped me succeed in the major leagues. It was discipline, and I learned it when I visited Cuba with him the first time. That trip was surreal. I saw where my father came from, how he grew up. For the first time, I spoke to my grandmother Teodora in person, not on the phone. Up until then I had been raised by my parents and my mom's side of the family.

Being in Cuba, it changed me. I learned not to take things for granted anymore. It opened my eyes to the sacrifices my dad had made and those that his dad had made. I thought about how my grandfather told my father to stay in the States during the Castro regime. He said, "Stay over there and train." Family is so important, but they both knew that they had to sacrifice. The times called for it, and they both had the discipline to accept that.

Knowing that, I knew I could never use anything as an excuse. Compared to them, the sacrifices I had to make were a piece of cake. I just wanted to persevere.

TP: I had no trouble raising my sons, Eduardo and Victor. We were in the United States and Puerto Rico by then. I was established in the big leagues. Plus, I was a lucky man. I married a woman who is a great mother to our kids.

I met my wife, Pituka, when I was in Puerto Rico in 1964. She is the best, my other half. We are always together. She raised Eduardo and Victor. She really did a great job on them. She would tell me that the kids were doing this and the kids were doing that. I was really lucky. She had been raised in a good family. Even now, she is the one who worries about everything in the family.

Now I get to be a grandfather. Every time we go to see Eduardo's girls, we take them out. We drive around and show them different places. We introduce them to different people. We want them to know everyone and everything, not just kids' stuff or what is taught in school. We want them to know how people live and how they do things. Afterward they ask, "Are we going back there? Are we going to take a ride?" I love when they ask me that.

Family is so important, but they both knew that they had to sacrifice. The times called for it, and they both had the discipline to accept that. Knowing that, I knew I could never use anything as an excuse. Compared to them, the sacrifices I had to make were a piece of cake.

EP: I am blessed. I get to spend a lot of time with my daughters. I love to wake up in the morning and take them to school. I love seeing them be active, riding their

Eduardo Pérez and daughters

bikes. We play on the weekends. I take them to the park and the beach, where they love to play in the sand. I also love that they speak two languages. My dad had to learn English later in life. Now I give that to my daughters. It is cool when I quiz my four-year-old in English. It reminds me what my father had to go through to get here. What he has done, the decision he made to leave Cuba and go it on his own, afforded me so much opportunity. So I pay it forward by spending as much time with my girls as I can.

TP: As a father, I wanted to see the boys grow and play and have fun. I did not focus on training them for sports. I knew that they could get big and strong just by playing the game. I never did anything other than that—except maybe running to school. When we were late my mother would yell, "Get out, get out, run!" That is how a kid should get his exercise.

EP: I grew up with television and Atari. We would play for a long time, but then dad would have enough of that. He would tell us to get out. "Go get your bikes and go outside," he would say. He didn't want us to play inside all the time. Now when he is around, he sees my girls playing their

Nintendo DS and just looks at me. That look says, "Don't let them be on that thing too long."

TP: I never tried to push the boys into playing baseball. I wanted them to have fun growing up. I wanted them to go and play the game. When the time came that Eduardo was ready to listen, then I talked to him. I didn't tell him what to do, though, because if you have the tools and the talent, you will play ball. For me, that is what happened. That's how I ended up leaving Cuba.

> *I wanted to see the boys grow and play and have fun. I did not focus on training them for sports. I knew that they could get big and strong just by playing the game.*

EP: I feel I had a big-time advantage because dad played in the majors. Dad never forced us into baseball, but we grew up at the ballpark. We went there with Dad and watched the game. We met the personalities, and that helped me love the game.

When I was little, Dad never came to see my Little League games. He didn't want other parents to put pressure on me. He saw all my basketball games, though. In fact, he saw a lot more basketball games when I was young than baseball games. Even then I knew how much he wanted to be there, to be just a dad watching his boy play ball. Looking back, I see that he sacrificed being at my games to make sure it stayed a game, not a job, for me.

Tony Pérez and family

TP: I watched some of Eduardo's games from the car in left field. No one knew I was there. I think about how Eduardo grew up. He would be at the ballpark with me, running around with Pete Rose Jr. and my other teammates' sons. They would go into the clubhouse and take all the gum. I was usually getting ready for the game, so I couldn't pay much attention to them.

EP: I remember being at the ballpark. How can I forget Bernie Stowe yelling, "Get out of here, you little sons of bitches!" Eventually I sent him a check for $500 to cover expenses for all the gum and anything else I may have done. He never cashed it, though.

Now I have my two little girls. One goes one way, one goes the other. You know what I learned from my dad, though? I will support whatever they have a passion for. One is four, the other is seven. The younger one loves ballet, and the older one loves tennis. I tell them, "You choose what you want to do, and I'll get you there."

Sometimes I stop and try to imagine what my grandparents must have felt when my dad decided to leave Cuba. I doubt my girls will be faced with something like that, but that doesn't mean I can't appreciate what that must have been like. They made a huge sacrifice for my dad, and my dad made a huge sacrifice for me that my daughters benefit from now. The least I can do is pay it back by being the best dad I can be. And in my heart, I know that if I was called upon to make a sacrifice for my family, I would not hesitate. Dad taught me that. My grandfather taught me that. I learned from their examples, and I would be proud to do that for my girls. When it comes right down to it, they are what life is all about.

When I was little, Dad never came to see my Little League games. He didn't want other parents to put pressure on me…. Looking back, I see that he sacrificed being at my games to make sure it stayed a game, not a job, for me.

Mike Golic | Pushing Trucks

Mike Golic is a former National Football League defensive lineman for the Houston Oilers, Philadelphia Eagles, and Miami Dolphins. He also played for the University of Notre Dame, where his two sons are on the football team together. He co-hosts ESPN Radio's Mike and Mike in the Morning. *His daughter is an accomplished swimmer.*

If you had driven down a road in Willowick, Ohio, back in the mid-'80s, you might have looked out your window and seen a couple of Golics pushing a truck. Not on the road or to help someone whose engine had stalled. No, in the middle of a field. It was part of our football conditioning—the brainchild of our dad, Lou Golic.

Dad worked us out each afternoon in the summer when I was in college. My brother Greg and I would lift in the morning and then wait for him to get home from work. He had a tough job as a bricklayer, but no matter how tired he was he would grab something to eat and take us out to the field.

Those workouts would go on for two hours sometimes. Dad would lay out the cones, and we would do agility and speed drills as well as push the truck around. Even when I came home from the University of Notre Dame with a workout regimen from the coaches, Dad would still put me through all of that.

I hated it! The only guy I ever played with who said he liked practice was Jim McMahon, and he wore the red shirt so no one hit him. During those times with my dad, we would work ourselves to exhaustion. I might end a sprint on my hands and knees throwing up, and Dad would give me a second to stand back up. Then we were back at it.

See, Dad was all about commitment. If back then I had said no to practice, he would not have forced me. He would have known that I wasn't serious about it. His philosophy was, "If you do it, you do it 100 percent." And if we did it 100 percent, he would be there helping us 100 percent. As long as we were committed, he was going to help us to be the very best we could be.

> *Dad was all about commitment…. His philosophy was, "If you do it, you do it 100 percent."*

What I didn't hate was the time we had with Dad. I might have taken it for granted back then—I thought every father did that kind of thing with his kids—but with age comes wisdom. Later on my brothers and I realized just how great our parents were.

With Dad, we definitely connected a lot through sports. My brothers and I have tons of stories about his exploits. One of our favorites was when my oldest brother, Bob, said he wanted to play football for the first time. Bob was in middle school at the time. Dad sat him down and told him all the things that could happen—punches, kicks, torn ligaments, the works. When Bob said he still wanted to play, my dad took him to practice at school. He walked up to the head coach and said, "Bob wants to play football. I am your new head coach." My dad was a big guy, so the coach said, "Sure thing."

Once we got together and asked dad about that story.

We said, "Why'd you do that, Dad?"

He said, "I figured I knew more than that guy about football."

Dad played football in the Canadian league for eight years, so he was probably right. But there was something wrong with his logic.

We asked, "Why did you coach us in baseball then?"

That got him, so he admitted he just wanted to coach. He said that if we were going to play, he wanted to get involved. That was the kind of father he was, very hands-on.

Dad is a former marine, too. It is not surprising he was very strict. He was a disciplinarian, a tough dad, but he was also fair. He was and is also our friend. Although on the practice field we may have taken him for granted, there is no doubt his help paid off.

I grew up in a very stable, very loving family. That is amazing, too, considering the size of my brothers and me. I still have no idea how they could afford to feed the three of us. I remember my mom making big dinners. We were all busy in sports, so we rarely had the chance to sit down all together. But you never wanted to be the last Golic boy home. If you were, dinner would usually be gone, and you had to make yourself a peanut butter and jelly sandwich—or six.

That was the kind of world I grew up in. My town was mostly middle- to lower-middle-class families. There were mostly two-parent families, and both parents usually had to work. At the same time, my parents were always around. I can't remember one of my sporting events when Dad didn't coach or Mom wasn't up in the stands.

Now I find myself being the exact same way with my kids. Like I said, with time comes wisdom. When I had a family, I looked back and saw how great an example my dad set. My wife and I try to get to every event my kids take part in. The imprint Dad made is very deep.

With time comes wisdom. When I had a family, I looked back and saw how great an example my dad set.

If you asked my wife to describe me as a father, I think she would say I am devoted. I have always been very involved with my kids. I am passionate about my sons'—Mike and Jake—football, and my daughter Sydney's swimming. Sometimes when I am talking them through something or trying to motivate them, I stop and chuckle because I have just said something my father shared with me when I was their age.

The way I see it, I was fortunate to have made it as a professional athlete. I want to impart everything I learned from that to my kids. Often I tell my sons that they will have to sweat, get hit, maybe even push a truck if football is really what they are passionate about. I tell my daughter that she might have to sacrifice a dance or time with her friends if swimming is what she wants. I never force them, but I have instilled that same sense of commitment that Dad instilled in me.

Mike Golic

When it came to motivating them for sports, it was not difficult. They were active kids. Even before playing anything organized, they were always doing something—rollerblading, hockey with the neighbors, anything that was active. Back then, kids still walked over to friends' houses and started a pickup game. Like my mom and dad, we never pushed the kids toward sports. We waited for them to show an interest, and we tried to expose them to as many experiences as we could.

Now I see a lot of parents steering their kids in certain directions. I understand how competitive the school scholarships are. Kids tend to veer toward one sport in the hopes of being good enough to earn one. Even coaches now tell kids not to play any other sport. I get that, but I think it is still better to let your kids choose what they are into and then just be there as much as you can. Get involved and show them that you care about what they are doing. Before you know it, the time you have with them will be gone.

The bottom line is that the very reason you have children is to be involved. No one is obligated to have kids. There is nothing wrong in making the decision not to. What I don't understand is when people decide to have children but decide not to spend that time with them. I am not talking about people who have to work 80 hours a week to make ends meet. There are parents out there who have the opportunity but not the right attitude. They think that coaches and schools are there to take care of their kids. That I do not get.

It is easy to get involved with your kids. When you're at home, just pick up a stick or a ball. I think a lot of the reason my kids were so active was that my wife and I were, too. When Mike and Jake were born, I was still playing football. They were in the locker room all the time with me. Sydney was born the year I retired, but she had a great role model in her mom, who is also athletic and very active.

Some parents think that coaches and schools are there to take care of their kids. That I do not get.

One of the greatest rewards I received from my kids being so active and into sports came when my sons decided to play football for the University of Notre Dame. You have to understand, I didn't grow up a fan of the Irish. Like I tell Greenie, my partner on the radio (Mike Greenburg), unlike him I was not a fan of any team growing up. I just played sports. When my brother Bob went to Notre Dame and then Greg followed him, I was more than happy to play there. For one thing, it meant playing on the same team as Greg again, which we did as kids. Once I got there, it became part of me, like it did for my brothers. I met my wife there; she went to Saint Mary's across the street. Now I bleed blue and gold.

As my sons were growing up, I noticed that they could really play football. I knew they grew up with all the Notre Dame stuff around the house, but I wanted them to be open to going where they wanted to go. I remember taking Mike Jr. to the University of Florida to meet [head coach] Urban Meyer. That night, we sat down to dinner.

I said, "It is about to start for you guys. I don't want you to go to Notre Dame because I played there. You are not supposed to live my life. I want you to take trips; go to other schools. I will not be mad. Blood is thicker than alumni status." I meant it, too. If he went to Nebraska, I would still love him. Maybe not USC, though—just kidding. I would still love him because he, like the other two, is my kid.

In the end it was in their blood. They really wanted to go to Notre Dame. After Mike committed, I told Jake that did not mean he had to go there. I gave him the same speech.

Afterward, he said, "If I get an offer from Notre Dame, I am going there. I want to play with my brother like we did in high school."

And now my daughter wants to go there, too. Honest, I had nothing to do with it!

So what else was there to do but cry when Mike ran out of that tunnel and onto the field for the first time? I did. My wife did, too. There I was, cheering for the entire team. Then Mike came out. I just stopped and looked. It was such a great experience. I thought it could not be topped.

The next year it was. I was in the stands for Notre Dame's home opener against Nevada. Both of my boys came running out together. The feeling I had the year before doubled. It was kind of an unreal experience. I can only imagine what it will be like watching Sydney swim there if she gets the chance.

All that makes me think back to when the boys used to run around in the locker room when I played. Now they are running around in their own locker room. If you were to ask my kids to describe me as a father, they would probably say I am too dedicated. I can imagine my sons thought exactly that when I had them in the basement the day after one of their high school games going over the film I had taken. All of my kids might say that when I start to talk, especially about sports, I talk a little too much. They might say, "Okay, we got it the third time."

I know something they don't, though. As I got older and had a family, I started to understand what my father had given me. And I am trying to give them the same thing. I have no doubt they will see that when the time comes. And maybe they'll have their kids out there pushing trucks, too.

Kirk Gibson | Clutch

Kirk Gibson is a former Major League Baseball player. Although he started his career with the Detroit Tigers, he is perhaps best known for his clutch home run as a Los Angeles Dodger in Game 1 of the 1988 World Series. He has three sons and a daughter.

It happens all the time, and did even when they were young. The kids and I would be watching television, usually a baseball game. Something would happen and the network would pull out the clip of their dad limping around the bases, pumping his fist. That clip has a life of its own. No doubt that home run has stuck with me, but maybe for a different reason than it has for the network.

Here is the setup. It was Game 1 of the 1988 World Series. My Los Angeles Dodgers were playing the Oakland Athletics. In the ninth inning, we were down 4–3 and there were two outs. Mike Davis was on first when Tommy Lasorda tapped me to pinch hit.

There was a reason I was available to pinch hit in the ninth. I had a stomach bug, and both my legs were injured. I really didn't think I was going to play at all that night. In the end though, as it often does in life, the opportunity presented itself.

Added to those injuries, I knew I was going to face one of the best closers of the time, Dennis Eckersley, with two outs in the ninth. I could have let the injuries and the quality of the opposition predetermine the outcome of my at-bat. I could have stayed on the bench and said I didn't have it. That would have been the path of least resistance. I was not going to let that happen, though. I reached down deep into my spirit for the game of baseball, a spirit that my father helped me grow to its fullest, and I stepped into the box.

I could have struck out, too. Considering the situation, the odds were probably good that would happen. If I did, it would have been okay, because when I walked onto the field, I already knew I was giving it everything I had. If I failed at that point, I could live with that fact. If I succeeded, though—what a reward!

Honestly, my mind-set was not "home run or bust." My immediate goal was to turn over the lineup. Steve Sax was up next, if I could just keep the game alive. Sure, I was open to getting a lucky one, as well.

Walking out, I heard the crowd roar. That is when I convinced myself I was not hurt. That didn't matter anymore. I let it rip and hit a walk-off home run to win the game. That hit personified what I am saying. It was my spirit playing the game I loved. It is that spirit that I hope to pass on to my kids. It is about failing and succeeding. It is about effort and reward. It showed itself in my sport, but it is something that you can carry throughout every aspect of your life. In a lot of ways, it is also the definition of parenthood.

When you enter parenthood for the first time, it can be daunting. You might feel something like both your legs hurting and the best closer in the game throwing bullets at you. At that moment, when you feel like you have no idea what to do, I think there is no better role model to look up to than your own father. Maybe there were things about your

When you enter parenthood for the first time, it can be daunting.

relationship with your mom or dad that you didn't like. If so, those are the things you can change. In my case, there was so much I liked about how I was raised that I wanted to give the same thing to my kids.

My parents grew up during the Depression. My dad once told me that he had to sell vegetables on the street to make ends meet for the family. Like so many other young men of that time, he served in World War II. In fact, he was on the USS *Missouri*, the ship on which the empire of Japan signed the Instrument of Surrender, ending the war.

After the war, he met my mother, Barbara. They were married and had three kids. I was the only boy. My mom was an educator, and she loved to direct plays at the local high school in East Lansing. My dad started out as a tax auditor for the state of Michigan. Later on, he went back to school to become an educator, too. He ended up becoming a math teacher.

As you can see, I came from a standard, three-squares-a-day, American family. We were very active and loved recreational sports like boating and camping. My mom or dad would fix us breakfast and run home in the afternoon to fix us lunch. All in all, we were a self-sufficient family.

Watching both my parents work hard but also make time for us definitely inspired me as a parent. When I had

Kirk Gibson's clutch moment

my children, I played a lot of baseball with them. I did it because I loved it, but I also did it because that was how I was brought up. Growing up, we were always swimming and wrestling around as a family. Now I do that as much as I can with my kids.

I always made time for my kids, regardless of my career. To this day, it is still a priority to me. I am always accessible, and I will always make the time if they need it. In my opinion, anyone who says he cannot do that is copping out. Come on! You don't have five minutes? I can't believe that. Even if you don't, take the one second you walk past your kids to give them a compliment. If you do that, you've improved their spirit.

> *Take the one second you walk past your kids to give them a compliment. If you do that, you've improved their spirit.*

To my parents, spirit was so important. Because of the Depression and then the war, my dad was not able to participate in sports when he was young. He made sure we did, though. It was football, baseball, and basketball. After lunch, he would throw me the football or shoot baskets with me. We were always having a catch. You cannot underestimate what that does for a kid, especially when it comes to sports. But it was more than that. I loved being with my mom and dad, and that love bled into whatever activity it was we were doing. So when they spent time playing sports with me, they passed on that love.

I try to do the same with my kids. I want to establish that spirit in them. With that comes a great attitude, too.

I think that helps to avoid the rebellious streak you see in kids, and it can do wonders for your relationship with them. If your relationship is good, then your kids will be more open to taking in the information and wisdom you have to offer.

In that way, my relationship with my father opened me up to learning from him. He made sure he taught me the fundamentals. For example, he was a stickler about me holding the football correctly. His teachings obviously paid off because when I played flanker for Michigan State, I had just one fumble in four seasons. For someone who did not have the opportunity to play many sports when he was young, he really was a great teacher.

Isn't that what parenthood is all about, being a good coach? I think about the great information I received from coaches like Sparky Anderson and Jim Leyland. I also think about all the mistakes. You acquire them both over time. Along the way, you prioritize them and then methodically pass on the good while avoiding the mistakes.

As long as you are coming from the right place, coaching can change someone's life. That is how it was for me with football and baseball. When I was at Michigan State, I was pretty sure I would play football after college. My coach came to me and said that I should play baseball for Michigan State my senior year. He thought that might increase my stock value when the NFL draft came around. I did it and ended up doing very well. When the time came to make a decision, I was drafted to play football by the Arizona Cardinals and baseball by the Detroit Tigers. I ended up choosing baseball. It made sense to me. I loved the game and, from a business perspective, I thought I could have a better career there than in football. That little suggestion, that wisdom passed on from my football coach, totally changed my life.

That is how it is with your kids, too. My youngest loves hockey. He is also a great baseball player. I tell him not to give up on baseball. Maybe he will stay in hockey, maybe not. But like my parents were for me, I want to be there for my son. I want to share the wisdom I've learned and help him see both sides so he can eventually make the right decision for himself.

Sometimes you have to let your kids fail. That is such an important lesson for all kids to learn. Success is so much about timing and seizing the right moments. As parents, we try to prepare them for that. At the same time, we have to help them learn how, in times of defeat, tofocus on the positive and take those good things as lessons to learn for the next time.

> *Success is so much about timing and seizing the right moments. As parents, we try to prepare them for that.*

That is why sports are so important to childhood. There is no better practice for life. Never again will concepts like winning and losing be so clear and unwavering. That is why athletics are such a perfect opportunity for parents to really get involved with their kids.

My dad was very intense in all things, including sports. He had great attention to detail and instilled in me the importance of relentless practice. As part of that, he and my mother both taught me that if I made a commitment like joining a team, I had to stand by it. They made sure I never missed practice. I was prompt and dedicated. Those are great lessons for every part of life.

When I was in ninth or tenth grade that there were kids who were better than me. I got very frustrated, and I just wanted to play more. My parents helped me to understand that I could not control what all those other people were doing. I could only control myself.

Once I was able to do that, it helped me focus on my game. In the end, I got the scholarship. Some of those kids who were better than I was did not. Had I simply focused on those kids, things could have ended up very differently.

That is why you teach your kids to never give up. I am a living example of that. Kids develop at different ages and in different ways. You never know how everything is going to shake out. My parents helped me grow up thinking that I didn't have to make it today because there was always tomorrow. In ninth grade, I struggled for playing time. Not long after that I won the Big Ten championship and a couple of World Series. I'd say it was well worth my time.

My three kids are athletic, too. I am happy about that because it allows me the opportunity to impart to them some of that wisdom my parents gave to me. The kids love hockey and baseball. They have dreams to make it big in sports. But if those dreams don't pan out, I know they have learned the skills that will translate to anything they decide to do. They have formed good habits that will help them succeed. Many of those habits ended up coming from athletics.

Giving your kids that option is so important. I could have pressed my kids toward sports and making it as a professional. That is the trap so many parents fall into; they want something more than their child does. When that is the case, it will never work out. Kids have to do what they want to do, and we have to expose them to everything we can so they can

By pointing, not pressuring, your children will find what they love.

find it. Our job is to point them in the right direction. By pointing, not pressuring, your children will find what they love. When they do, they will have the spirit to be successful at it.

I think back to that home run in Game 1 of the 1988 series. I had my share of failures leading up to that. One home run and it was all better. That epitomizes the lessons my father taught me. As opposed to getting down on yourself when you fail, look forward to the next time you get the chance to succeed. That is what being clutch is all about. You always have another chance to succeed.

When I was playing ball as a kid, I remember my mom and dad instilling that concept in me. I remember doing something in a Little League game, making a great play that influenced the game, and my parents celebrated that. It imprinted in me the desire to succeed. It was that desire that I've leaned on when I failed.

I've tried to do the same with my kids. I hope they have the spirit to do something that they dream about. I hope they know that failure is okay, too. I hope they can see that they will never know how good they can be until they put everything on the line. I tried my best to pass on my parents' wisdom to them. There were times I failed as a parent. There were times I got frustrated. But when I made a mistake, I kept going forward. That is the spirit of parenthood, and we all need to keep that spirit alive. In the end, we are all one swing away from immortality.

Steve Garvey | Full Circle

Steve Garvey is a former Major League Baseball player. A ten-time All-Star and a National League MVP, Garvey played for the Los Angeles Dodgers and San Diego Padres. His father drove a charter bus for the Dodgers during spring training from the time Steve was a child until the day Steve left the Dodgers in 1982.

One day, my dad came home and asked me if I had any tests the next day. I said I didn't, and he asked if I wanted to skip school. I was shocked. Dads, especially back then, did not ask you if you wanted to skip school. Then he told me that he had a charter to pick up the Brooklyn Dodgers at the Tampa airport and take them to a spring game against the Yankees. I could not believe it. Not only was I able to meet the Brooklyn Dodgers, I ended up becoming a batboy for the team—all thanks to my dad.

Dad was a big old bear of a guy. He was 6'3" and more than 240 pounds. He had big hands and played tackle in high school and in semipro football on Long Island with my uncle, who was a big guy, too. Dad was a likable man, very soft spoken. He was so personable; I never knew anyone who didn't like him.

He was perfect for his job. He was a Greyhound bus driver. As a service job, it was all about interacting with people. His personality fit that perfectly. He was just a gentle giant of a guy. He was a great example, not only as a father, but as a person. The day I was born, he realized how big a responsibility it would be to be a father. He looked at me and said, "That looks like a lot of work, so let's just have one."

Having been an athlete himself, he enjoyed sports. So it's not surprising that he and a few other gentlemen started the first Little League in Tampa, Florida. It was called Drew Park Little League. The age requirement was eight years old. I was seven and a half, but they were short on kids, so I started early.

He had one rule. If you start something, you finish it. For sports, and that meant showing up for all the practices, all the games, plus practicing on the side. The uniform was kept clean, and it was worn the right way. You said, "Yes, sir," to the coach, and you played hard all the time. Most important, you enjoyed it. That's what Dad expected.

My dad had one rule. If you start something, you finish it.

Those are pretty simple expectations, and I kept them as a parent myself. People ask me what kind of rules and discipline I had as a kid. As you can see, they were pretty simple. It was my parents making a commitment to me and in turn asking me to take responsibility and see it through to the end.

My mother actually was more the disciplinarian. She was the secretary for the president of an insurance company. She was a pretty smart gal, and she was a good balance to my dad. He would talk things through with me. He might scold me, usually gently, and tell me what I should do. He'd tell me to try not to make the same mistake twice. Mom, on the other hand, was a little more vocal.

Growing up, my dad played with me through sports. He bought me my first glove, and we would have a catch. We would throw the football and play basketball. I'd say that 95 percent of our interactions were sports related. That's the way it was back in the '50s and '60s.

I like to say that life was seasonal back then. You went from baseball season to football season to basketball season. Life seemed like it was a team sport. Nowadays, sports have changed, much like life has. It is more focused and intense. Kids play a single sport now. If a kid tries something, likes it, and shows a little bit of talent, he or she will probably not just do the traditional school or recreational league. He or she will get into travel or academy sports.

It was a simpler time back then, and it was probably more fun. We had sandlots. We got out and played catch with Dad. Now everything is so scheduled. Practice is three nights a week, games are out of town, and kids are always on the go. I think that has changed the way kids interact with their parents today.

One of my most nostalgic childhood memories with my dad was breaking in a glove with him. We had the saddle soap and the Rawlings Glovolium. We'd submerge the glove in water and then throw some Glovolium in it. Then I would put two balls inside and tie it closed with a clean sock. Within two or three days, the glove would be dry. After untying it and taking out the balls, you would have a pretty neat pocket to begin with. But back then, gloves were a lot stiffer than they are now.

It was a simpler time back then, and it was probably more fun. We had sandlots. We got out and played catch with Dad. Now everything is so scheduled.

From our time around the Dodgers, we knew how to do stuff like that—how to break in a glove, how to take care of a bat, what to put on your shoes…all these little things. It was an adventure for Dad and I to be around a Major League team, to see the things they did. I learned how to look like a ballplayer and even how to fold my hat just right.

It was March of 1956 the first time my dad got the charter to drive the Dodgers during spring training. They really liked the job he did. Lee Scott, the traveling secretary, would give him a $50 tip after dad dropped off the players at the airport. I remember him saying, "Hey Joe, you did a great job for us. We'll ask for you next time." My dad said, "Absolutely." From then on, every spring through my final year with the Dodgers, 1982, Dad drove the bus when the Dodgers came to the Tampa area from the West Coast. I was a batboy from 1956 to 1963. By

Steve Garvey and his father, Joe

then, I was more active in baseball, and that cut into my time.

It was really a charming story. There I was, a seven-year-old kid, able to batboy for the Dodgers because of my dad. Then when I got older, I was drafted by the Dodgers. On my first spring training trip east, there is my dad, picking up me and the rest of the team at the airport. From 1969 until I went to the Padres, I was a Dodger. And the "bussy," that's what we called him, was my dad. Sounds like a Hollywood script, but for me it was just a neat experience to share with my dad.

I learned so much during that time. From the players I looked up to, I chose virtues I thought were important to life. When I think about my dad, he was the one who taught me some of the greatest virtues. He taught me to believe in God and to respect other people. He showed me a good work ethic. He taught me sportsmanship, teamwork, and the importance of giving back.

He instilled in me that I was given a gift and that I should truly appreciate it by sharing it with others—maybe

Being verbal is important, but living your life that way is what passes on the message.

by teaching a kid to field a grounder or by having a terminally ill child visit the dugout and making that child's life more important than my own for that hour and a half.

He set a great example. He didn't just talk it, he lived it. I have always thought that is the essence of good leadership. Being verbal is important, but living your life that way is what passes on the message.

Dad was a charter driver as opposed to having a standard route. He chose that so he had the flexibility to come see me play. Because the games were Friday nights, he rarely missed a football game. When he was off other times he would come and watch practice. He would be one of two dads sitting in the stands. He never said anything and never bothered the coaches.

One of the greatest compliments I heard was when a coach came up to me and said, "You know, of all the dads I've ever dealt with, yours is the best. He doesn't tell me my job and doesn't tell me what to do. He's just there to support you and the program." You absorb that as a son, and you think that is how you want to parent someday.

When it came to deciding on a career in baseball, my dad's philosophy was, "As long as you want to play something, we are there to support you." As time went on, football and baseball were my strengths, so we decided not to play basketball after my junior year. There were more and more scouts coming to the games to watch me play. I was drafted by Minnesota after my senior year, but I really wanted to go to college. I was going to be the first one in the family to do that. I had 20 or 25 offers from schools like Florida, Florida State, and Auburn, but they were mostly for either baseball or football. I had three or four that would let me play both. That's what I wanted to do, so I chose Michigan State.

It was great having that kind of relationship with my dad. I knew I could talk to him. We always talked things through. We would make decisions together and try to put as much logic in it as possible. Looking back at it, I cannot tell you how lucky I was to have a dad like that.

If you think about it that way, it is no wonder I became a ballplayer. My early life was about living the game. When I was seven, I got to be a batboy, and then two weeks later I played my first Little League game. I didn't understand a lot of what was going on that first spring when I sat next to Jackie Robinson and Pee Wee Reese. Spring after spring, the more I played baseball, the more I understood. I watched those players, and each year I learned more from what I saw. It is one thing to read a book. Every Little League coach will teach you something different. When you sit on the bench and listen to the pros talk about tipping pitches and stealing signs, which were part of the game back then, those lessons were unbelievable. They would be able to tell what pitch was coming by the way the pitcher held the ball or moved his glove. I picked up these kinds of things through osmosis.

This was in 1956, when the Dodgers first won the Series. It was an amazing team. They had a quiet confidence— they were a group of people who had come from very different places but had one shared goal. That's why so many people have written books about them. They had a tremendous amount of character and charisma—maybe more than the Yankees did at the time.

As time went on, I was pretty blessed to be around them and to learn things that took years as an advanced player to understand. Just watching how Reese would get the sign and how he would give it to Robinson. Just before the pitch, he would move over and you would know it was a breaking ball to a lefty. That experience might be why I was only in the minor leagues for two years. I had a great grasp of the game and was able to take advantage of the things given to me by the opposing team. It was like I entered the minors when I was 12 or 13 years old.

Athletics are so much more sophisticated now. In my day, you used baseball equipment to get into baseball shape. You threw the ball and ran the bases. It was all part of preparing for the game. Now there is so much more to it. There are supplements, and there is strength training. Boys and girls are bigger and stronger and faster today, but maybe they are not trained to be better baseball players. Fundamentals do not hold the importance they once did.

If you took a picture of a young athlete today and compared it to a picture of an athlete from twenty years ago, they are structurally different. Does that mean today's athlete plays the game better? I don't necessarily think so. The thing I hear nowadays from minor-league directors is that these superior athletes make it to the majors faster, but when they get there they don't know the game like the players used to.

Now sports for kids are structured. I think this is due to the evolution of competitive sports. Travel and academy teams are influenced by the fact that the economics of sports have changed so much. I see it with my son, who plays for an academy baseball team. For a family today with a kid who shows potential, their biggest investment in life may be that child. When a child plays on a travel team, there are costs such as registration, equipment, and travel expenses. There are showcases and tryouts. The end reward is so great that parents are willing to do anything in the hope that their kid is the one who makes it to the majors and gets that average salary of $3 million a year.

It starts so young now. I would like it to be simpler at an early age. Before kids are 11 or 12, it is hard to tell what kind of athlete they will be. Before that, they may have just matured faster than the other kids. Also, there is no way of knowing if they are going to like it and be committed enough to do what they have to do to try to make it as a pro.

With my sons, I wanted someone else to work with them so they heard another voice. I watched closely what and how the coaches were teaching, but I didn't coach and sponsor their teams until they were 12 years old. That's not to say that I wasn't anxious watching them.

I have talked to a lot of former professional athletes about what it is like to be the father and watch your kid play. We are all in a fraternity, I think. It is inherently human that you want your kids to do well. For me, it is more important that he plays the game the right way and that he respects the coaches and other players. I always tell him, "I have the answers to the test. Just listen to me," and he laughs.

For the kids, there is added pressure. When people see the name Garvey on their backs, there is an expectation. So we talk about it a lot. We talk about how much of a blessing my career was and about giving back. My son keeps it in pretty good perspective. I tell him, "You don't necessarily have to have a part in your hair," but we have to realize those expectations and respect the game.

Travel has really helped him. He has had to go around the country and experience people recognizing who he is. That's helped him to deal with it. It is all part of the psychology of the game. It is so important that he keeps enjoying it. If there comes a time that he doesn't, he needs to change gears and go on to different things.

The whole process is one that becomes very consuming these days. I see how important it is to parents. Sometimes it is so paramount in the family that they forsake other children or other responsibilities. It is all about their son or daughter making it. A lot of times decisions are made for dollars and cents instead of what is best for the child.

> *A lot of times decisions are made for dollars and cents instead of what is best for the child.*

I can see the pressure. My son was the starting first baseman of his high school team. There were a lot of expectations at the beginning of the season, but it started out slowly. He strained his back a little bit. He struggled and was down to fifth or sixth in the batting order. He was pretty down, and I tried to talk to him about the psychology of slumps. It is tough. You can say all you want, but if you are the guy in the slump, it is tough.

It was a very windy night in Palm Desert, California, and he was not going to start. I said to him, "You know, Ryan, just sit out this game. Get ready for the next one."

So the team got off to a good start. They had four runs by the third. The wind was howling, and dust was flying. A couple kids were on base, and the coach pinch hit for the eight hitter, probably thinking if Ryan got a hold of one, the game would be over. So Ryan stepped up and he looked over at me. He gave me a shrug, saying, "I'm in here kind of early, huh?"

I mouthed the words, "Just let it go."

Well, the first pitch, he just let it go. He hit it about 390 feet over the left-field fence. At home plate, he looked at me and put his hands up. I said, "Attaboy."

There was only one out at the time. The team was hot and we got a few more runs, and Ryan got to the plate again with a few kids on. First pitch, he takes it 400 feet dead center. He had five RBIs and two home runs. At home plate, he shrugged again. I was out-of-my-skin excited for him.

We had been talking about how baseball was like life. Sometimes things do not go perfectly. We all get in slumps, and we have to keep our heads up and take responsibility for it. I told him, "If you keep swinging and keep working on it, you'll get out of it." That's what he did.

After the game, he came up. He dropped his bag and we hugged and smiled. He patted me on the head—he's taller than me. It was a defining moment for him. He understood what I was talking about. In life, when things aren't going well, it is so easy to blame other people. In life, we are always going to be challenged. And we are the authors of our own destiny.

Things are going to go wrong, but if you stay the course, take responsibility, and stay aggressive then every slump will come to an end. It may be with just a dribbler down the third-base line. In fact, most slumps do end that way.

Not all kids are the same, though. My little one is night to his brother's day. I remember one of his football games. He ran down a guy who was faster than he was in the last play of his football season in the quarterfinals. The guy was clearly in the open. Somehow my son chased him down and jumped on his back. He got up and did a little dance. His teammates were trying to jump on him, but he ran right past them. He took his helmet off and ran toward the sidelines where his mother and I were standing. He passed her and jumped right on me. Literally, he almost knocked me over. It was just the joy of having done something more than what was expected of him.

Having boys is so much different than having girls. I have four older daughters. They are in New York, Washington, and Los Angeles. Every day I talk to at least two of them. They are doing this or that. There are so many more semantics with them. The boys are more literal. If there is a

"Big Joe" and Steve Garvey

problem, we just go shoot baskets or go to the batting cage. We talk it out there. With the girls, you have to be fatherly. You have to act like you don't understand but still give good advice.

For a father, it is the same thing my dad did. Expose your kids to whatever their interests are. Buy them the best equipment you can. Support them and make the one rule—if you start something, you finish it. After each season, the kids decide if they want to continue.

You love them. You nurture them. And you have to let them fail. Then you talk them through it, prop them up, and let them go on their own. We tell the girls, "You're adults now. We can't be there for every problem you have. You have to swim. But we will never let you sink."

The older girls all did some activity, sports, or jazz band. There were no softball players until my 15-year-old. They went to all my games, though. They grew up at Dodger Stadium. They learned it was a great way to attract cute boys.

> *We tell the girls, "You have to swim. But we will never let you sink."*

In the end, I think sports are wonderful. They are the thread that weaves together our society, from what you learn to the entertainment and the business of it. If your child does not have the talent or interest for it, find what does interest him or her. There are professional athletes who have children who are not athletic, so they support them in what they do want to do.

I think back to my dad and that first day chartering the Dodgers. There is no doubt that shaped me. Amazingly, he drove that bus until I left the Dodgers. It was such a great experience and such a great story. Not every dad will have an opportunity like that. That's why you have to seize what you can and just spend that time with your kids. It will come full circle in the end, and it will shape everything they do from this day forward.

Amy Van Dyken | The Challenges You Overcome

Amy Van Dyken is an Olympic gold medalist. She has earned six gold medals in swimming, four during the 1996 Games in Atlanta, Georgia. She suffers from severe asthma. She took up swimming upon a doctor's advice as a possible treatment.

I had my first asthma attack at around 10 months. Eight months later I was diagnosed with three forms of the disease—exercise-induced, allergy-induced, and infection-induced asthma. I spent up to two weeks each month in the hospital and nearly died more than a few times. There was a commercial out not too long ago that showed a gold-fish out of water, its mouth gaping open painfully, its little eyes bulging. That's pretty much what it feels like to suffer from asthma. It never really hurt. It felt more like the fat guy from the circus was sitting on my chest and covering my nose and mouth at the same time.

Most often it would start slowly, but it would get worse and worse. The problem I had was that I wouldn't tell anyone. I am very stoic when it comes to wanting to draw that kind of

Amy and her mother

attention to myself. It was especially bad during the holidays because we would be on the go and I wouldn't want to ruin anyone's fun by complaining or saying I could not keep up. I never wanted to be different. Regardless, I had a pretty normal childhood. I have my parents to thank for that.

My parents are polar opposites. My dad is 6'4". He is a stern man and a disciplinarian. If I did something wrong and needed to be punished, he would take me upstairs for a spanking, but he would never hit me. It was then that my father's true side showed. He would smack his own leg, making a loud sound, and tell me to cry out.

There is no doubt he was the more serious one. If I fell off the track I was on, he would question me. But he was a great dad, and he never pushed me into anything. He let me do my own thing and simply loved me.

My mom, on the other hand, was just plain cool. She was that awesome mom that all the neighborhood kids wanted to have. Every day when I got home from school, she would have freshly baked cookies. We would sit down, and I would eat cookies while telling her about my day. She claims she is tall at 5'8" inches. I am 6'0", so I say 5'8" is nothing.

I had the best childhood ever. As severe as my asthma was, I was outside playing with Mom and Dad almost every day. We would build tree houses, play soccer, or just roll down a hill. They did everything they could so I could have a childhood like everyone else's. What they ended up giving me was even better.

When I think back, I can almost picture the time I spent with them. I remember we had this perfect crabapple tree. It was in the backyard and looked huge to me when I was young. Dad said that I couldn't climb it until I got older and strong enough. When I turned six, the day finally came and he told me it was time; that was the best day ever. The tree did not disappoint. Even better is the memory of my dad, all six and a half feet of him, up in that tree. It was hilarious.

It is amazing really that my childhood was so active. We used to go on these picnics. After lunch, we'd play baseball. I would hit, my mom would pitch, and my dad would be in the outfield. It was a lot of fun, but it also really represented what growing up was like for me.

> *As severe as my asthma was, I was outside playing with Mom and Dad almost every day. We would build tree houses, play soccer, or just roll down a hill.*

My parents put me in every single sport. I played softball, soccer, and volleyball. I ran track and did gymnastics. It was not always easy. Exercising caused me serious trouble. A lot of the time with sports like soccer, I was outside so my allergies would make it even worse.

There were definitely times when I felt a little different, too. I would have to sit out on a drill or something like that, and the kids at that age couldn't understand that. My parents did everything they could to smooth things out, and sometimes other people got involved.

I remember a pretty cool story from elementary school. The kids did not understand why I didn't do gym every day like they did. One of them told me that I didn't look sick. The gym teacher overheard and called everyone together. He pulled a kid out of the crowd and told him to run around the gym once. The kid did it, stopping beside the teacher, who took the microphone and put it up to the kid's mouth. Everyone heard his breathing.

Then the teacher told me to do the same thing. I ran around the gym and came back. When he put the microphone near my mouth, everyone could finally hear why I was different. Strangely, by pointing that out, it made me feel more a part of the class than I had before.

When I was six and my doctor suggested that swimming might help the asthma, my parents jumped at the idea.

My illness scared my parents. So when I was six and my doctor suggested that swimming might help the asthma, they jumped at the idea. They were very excited, immediately signing me up for the neighborhood pool's swim team. That expanded to include synchronized swimming and diving, as well. I think they hoped one or all of those things would be a magic cure.

It was not as if I was just thrown into the pool for the first time. I had always taken to water and had been in lessons since I was a little kid. That didn't mean that swimming came easily to me, though. Although the basics were natural, my asthma made it so I could barely paddle 12 yards before being dangerously out of breath. It took me six years of being on the team before I could swim a lap.

Even before I was finishing races, swim team was awesome. I would be outside, hanging out with my friends, eating Jell-O powder out of the box. I pretty much lived at the pool, which was great. The lifeguards were hot. What's not to like?

Before long, I was just like them. I competed and finished races. Even considering the reason I got into the sport, I never felt like I was swimming for my life or anything like that. It just was what it was. I thought it was fun, and I always loved the water.

For my parents, it may have been different. They probably felt that as long as I kept on swimming, my asthma might go away. I think they thought of it as a cure. My father had asthma as a young kid but grew out of it. So they always clung to that hope. But mine was so severe that I kind of knew it was a slim chance, if that.

Like I said, swimming competitively started out slowly for me. I remember finishing my first race at 12. Then when

I won my first race I got addicted, but I was not competitive until my junior year in high school. By senior year, I qualified for the 1992 Olympic trials. I remember winning the race and then hearing the announcement of my qualifying time. Kids came up to me and asked for my autograph. It was amazing.

When my parents heard that, they were excited that I had the chance to make the team. When I got to the Olympic trials, I finished fourth. I was disappointed, but my parents were so excited again. I couldn't figure that out, but then I realized that it was pretty incredible. It had not been that long before I could not even finish a lap. I had almost died a few times. In their minds, I might not have been alive to go to those trials.

In 1996 I made it to the Olympics in Atlanta. After I won the 50 in freestyle, I was quoted as saying, "This is a victory for all the nerds." To me, even to this day, a nerd is someone who does not fit in with everyone else. They march to the beat of their own drum and do not care about societal pressures. I could relate to that.

Although early on my teammates were great, I didn't have a lot of friends in high school. By junior year, it had even bled into sports. When I was not a good swimmer, the team kind of looked at me like "oh, little Amy." The kids all talked to me and were very nice. Then I started to beat them in races. They did not like that at all, and they did not handle it well. Here was this kid who wasn't good and couldn't practice as well as they could, and she should not be winning. At the same time, with my

Amy and her father

asthma, swimming a 50-meter was like a normal person swimming a 200.

Asthma may have put me in that box, but it might have been the fact that I was a skinny, 5'10" freshman with frizzy hair and glasses. In that moment when I won the gold, I thought about a lot of the kids who have been in my position. Maybe they were not the most athletic or the smartest. I thought about the kids who got harassed like I did, and I thought about that vision of the perfect Olympic athlete, beautiful and popular. I wanted kids who grew up like me to know that it was not always like that. You grow up, move on, and can still become whatever you want to be.

The truth is that if I could change anything in my life, it would not be my asthma. Because I had it, I became a good athlete. I wanted to prove people wrong. I am stubborn, and when someone tells me I cannot do something, I get pissed off. I remember I was on a relay once when I was still struggling as a swimmer. The other kids didn't want me on it. I remember thinking, "Who are you to think that?" That just lit a fire under me. Heck, if you told me today that I couldn't solve a crossword puzzle, I would stay up 48 hours straight just to prove you wrong.

My journey as an athlete really culminated when I was inducted into the Olympic Hall of Fame. When I received the announcement of my nomination, I was like, "You have got to be kidding me." I actually thought someone was playing a prank on me. So I checked it on the Internet and found out it was real. Even then, I didn't put together a campaign to try to get votes. I thought about all the amazing athletes who were nominated with me and those who were already in the hall, and I was a little embarrassed. It was hugely flattering, but I felt like I didn't deserve it.

When I got in, it was amazing. I thought about what my parents would think and how they would act. They had sacrificed so much for me. They had been plagued with their share of worry. At the same time, they did everything right.

If I were to give advice to parents who are struggling to raise active children, I think I would say, "Don't let them limit themselves." If they shoot for the moon, maybe they'll fall short and land on a star. If kids have asthma, diabetes, or some other challenge, don't let that define them. Keep on plugging away. You and your kids will have days when you want to quit, but so will everyone else. It is too easy to be defined by the challenges you have to overcome as opposed to overcoming them.

You and your kids will have days when you want to quit, but so will everyone else. It is too easy to be defined by the challenges you have to overcome as opposed to overcoming them.

I think my parents would give the same advice. They would say, "Don't let it stop you." I know that they were scared an awful lot of times, but that is part of being a parent. You help kids grow and become the best they can be. Holding them back will not enable that to happen. It will just make them afraid.

My parents spent so much time with me. We were always hanging out. We had family dinners almost every night. That's how I know that there is always enough time to spend with your kids. We all work hard to put money in the bank for our future. Well, kids are actually our future, and they are worth the investment. You brought them into the world for a reason. Spend time with them, and learn from them. They are so innocent and amazing. The things they know and can do make you a better person.

I know all this firsthand. My health may have been a challenge to overcome, but my parents filled the void and then some. The funny thing is that to them swimming was this magical cure that just did not deliver. To me it was a cure. Everything my parents did for me was a cure. Sure, it didn't take my asthma away, but like I said, I wouldn't change that for the world. What it did do was give me a normal life. They helped me become active, they supported everything I did, and that gave me the most incredible life I ever could have imagined. Thanks, Mom and Dad. You are awesome.

Jim Craig | Sacrifice

Jim Craig was the goalie of the 1980 U.S. Olympic hockey team that defeated the Soviet Union in one of the most memorable sporting events in history. He also played in the NHL for the Atlanta Flames, Boston Bruins, and Minnesota North Stars. He is the father of a daughter and a son.

It never gets old. Even today adults approach me and say something like, "Talking to you is a pretty big thing for me. As a kid, I pretended to be you when I was playing hockey in the backyard." That is awesome to me, but not in the sense of pride or vanity. What I love about it is that our team, the success we had in the 1980 Olympics, inspired kids to play.

February 22, 1980, was the day we beat the Soviet hockey team in the 1980 Winter Olympics. Since then, our story became about something much more than hockey. It became a symbol of triumph during a very difficult time in our country. Hostages were being held in Iran, Vietnam had ended badly, and the Cold War was at its peak. At

Jim and J.D. Craig

that moment, we found ourselves facing the juggernaut of hockey, the Soviet Olympic team. At a time when amateurs still took to the ice for the Olympic Games, we were facing some of the best professionals on the planet.

While we were in it I didn't see it that way. Over time, I learned that the game had more meaning. I knew going in we were representing our country in the game of hockey. That meant a great deal to me. It was an awesome responsibility for a group of kids. I knew about communism—everyone did. We all knew we were playing against pros that day. Every day since, however, I have learned from people just how important that moment was for them.

That game was only one moment from the 1980 Olympics. Throughout our run, we had 20 of the most unselfish guys with whom I have had the opportunity to compete.

We all shared a single dream and worked really hard at our jobs to achieve it. We supported each other and played as one from the first game through the gold medal round. We knew we were facing a team that had already beaten the NHL All-Stars. It was considered to be the greatest hockey team in the world. I remember how Jim McKay, the voice of the Olympics and *ABC*'s *Wide World of Sports*, put it. He said we were like a bunch of high school football players beating the vaunted Pittsburgh Steelers of the late 1970s.

There is no doubt that the climax of our journey was that battle against the Soviets, although it culminated for most of us when we stood on the podium after beating Finland for the gold. Herb Brooks said of seeing the entire team on the top of the podium, "That was the period, the chapter, the verse, the end of the story for me right then." None of it could have happened any other way, considering the social climate of the time. The game itself did not disappoint. It had all the makings of a classic, with comebacks, great defense, and an electrifying lead change in the third period. Those things combined, and the moment has resonated far more than I had thought it would at the time. Being part of a team that helped a country feel better was really important.

After the joyous team scrum on the ice following the clock striking 00:00 against Finland, I pulled myself up from the bottom of the pile, and within seconds a fan put an American flag on my shoulders. Draped in Old Glory, I skated toward the section of the stands where my father had been jumping up and down, pounding his feet, clenching his fists—never sitting calmly—during the game. The flag was now around my waist, but I held it tight to make sure it didn't touch the ice. A television camera fixed on me as I looked up into the seats, trying to find my best friend, the words, "Where's my father?" easily readable on my lips. Where was he? Then at my side was Leslie, fiancée of my teammate Mark Johnson. Leslie knew where my father was, and she pointed him out. I found him. We found each other.

That moment was so important to me. I just wanted to show respect to my father. I knew he was thinking about my mother, who had passed, and I wanted him to know that I was, too. All it took was a nod of the head. I didn't have to say anything. It was a moment of reflection and appreciation. It was all out of respect.

In life, people talk about personal sacrifices. Often they are referring to the ones they make for themselves. What gets lost are the sacrifices other people make for you. I could not have gotten to the Olympics without the personal sacrifices of others, especially my mother and father.

In life, people talk about personal sacrifices. Often they are referring to the ones they make for themselves. What gets lost are the sacrifices other people make for you.

I had four older sisters, an older brother, and two younger brothers. Mom and Dad had a lot of responsibilities in the way of feeding, clothing, and sheltering. They never had a day off, and day after day they were wonderful providers. While we may not have had a lot of

Jim Craig and his father

material wealth, we had enough, and our parents made sure we always knew an abundance of love and warmth and tenderness.

Some people I have spoken to find it amazing that I thought to seek out my father in the stands. The funny thing is that to me it was not amazing at all. That is the relationship we had, my father and I. My mother died in September 1977, just prior to my returning to BU for my junior year. The relationship between my father and me became even closer.

Then again, my dad and I were always close. In fact, he was the best man at my wedding. That was one of the easiest decisions I ever had to make. To me, it was not your "best friend" but your "best man." I could not think of anyone who came close to taking that title away from my dad.

In terms of hanging out with siblings, because we were close in age, my brothers Kevin and Danny and I were tight in playing sports and roughhousing. We were outside a lot. We had friends. We went to their houses, and they came to our house. We went all over the neighborhood and to the local park together. Back then, it was more of a community. We played Wiffle ball, baseball, hockey, basketball, kill the man with the ball (similar to rugby), and king of the hill. We built and raced go-carts.

The basement of our house saw a lot of activity; it was kind of spartan actually. We had a hockey goal set up down there, and I would defend it against shot after shot from my brothers and our buddies. We also lined up a couple of mattresses against the wall of the basement into which we would check one another to simulate getting checked into the boards when on skates and on ice. (We figured the trauma of hitting a mattress with no pads was about the same as getting slammed against the boards while wearing pads.)

But some of the best times were playing with Dad when he came home. My dad was the director of food services for a local junior college. He worked long hours and seven days a week during the school year. He also held part-time jobs, like serving on our town's board of health for more than 30 years (most of that time as chairman), and he volunteered as a youth sports coach. Interestingly enough, he never coached me in hockey.

Even though he was busy, especially during the school year, my dad made sure to give each of us quality time every day. Summers were great because he had more time at home, and when he was home he was always playing with us. I remember when my brothers and I would wait for him to get home. The front entrance to the neighborhood had two pillars. We would sit up there until we saw his car coming. Once it was in sight, we would race home. He could barely get out of the car before he had a bat or glove or basketball in his hands.

> *Even though he was busy, especially during the school year, my dad made sure to give each of us quality time every day.*

Once we got him out of the car, we would be in the backyard. He built a mound and a home plate back there. I usually pitched to him, and he would hit the ball to my brothers out in the field. He had great bat control and could send fly balls or grounders anywhere he wanted to.

Although it was hard to pull stuff out of Dad, I did learn that he had been a great athlete when he was young. He captained his high school basketball and football teams. He ran track, and he was drafted to play baseball for the Chicago Cubs. Unfortunately, while in high school he worked for a company that made shovels for the railroad. One day, one of the machines crushed his hand. Although he was still able to play sports with us, that ended his chances of playing professional ball. Being the man he was he never let that keep him down, and it just added to how much he liked to spend time teaching us the game.

When I took an interest in hockey, particularly in becoming a goaltender, he used his baseball skills to help train me. He had to because he could not skate. So he would put me against the backstop at a nearby park and hit baseballs and softballs at me. I would block them like I was defending the net. It really helped me develop soft hands and quick reactions.

All of that practice was wonderful, but one of the most valuable things my mother and father instilled in me was the importance of passion. Winning and losing mattered, but they were not the most important thing. Winning was a reward for embracing the passion for the game and competition. You played the game because you loved it and because you wanted to be the best you could possibly be.

Back then, my dad never had to talk to us about physical fitness or staying active. It was a different generation. We were active. If weather permitted, we were outside—both Mom and Dad insisted on that. And we stayed outside "until the streetlights came on." (Hockey practice in the basement was for when the weather was nasty or when it was dark out.) Again, I was fortunate to have two younger brothers, and we played together all the time. Also, because Dad was a food services director, we had a pretty good knowledge of how to eat healthy. It was all about balanced meals and moderation.

> Back then, my dad never had to talk to us about physical fitness or staying active. It was a different generation.

For my kids, instilling a healthy lifestyle through activity was not hard either. They love to compete, and I love to get out there and play with them. I still do it all the time. When they were little, I would get out the Nerf and throw it in the family room. My son J.D. would go out for passes and make diving catches into the couch. My daughter Taylor would compete with him.

I also loved coaching their sports teams. It was such a great way to be close to them, and athletics are such an important part of life. They teach teamwork, sportsmanship, goal setting, and healthy competitiveness. It leads to memorable moments of success, as well as how they react when they compete and lose. You learn so much about your kids when you watch them after a win or a loss.

Some of my fondest memories of my kids when they were young revolved around sports. J.D. is now 21, but I often think back to when I got him his first baseball glove. I will never forget watching my daughter play on the boys' varsity hockey team as a freshman. (Her brother was captain of the team.) Sports provided me with some of the best opportunities to just be there with them. Athletics can be a great bridge between parents and their kids, and today they also play an important role in ensuring kids stay healthy.

In the end, parenting is even more than that. Becoming a parent in the first place is an awesome responsibility and an incredible gift. Those two facets should never be forgotten or underestimated. You do not have a child for him or her to be raised by a nanny. Parenthood is not a

> *Becoming a parent in the first place is an awesome responsibility and an incredible gift.... Parenthood is not a status symbol.*

status symbol. Parenthood is about creating a legacy of the right values and direction.

Every day with your kids is as important as the next. I tried to enjoy and appreciate every one. It can be hard. There is no doubt that life likes to get in the way, but my calendar is about my kids. I make time for them whenever I can.

At the same time, we cannot live vicariously through them. Their life is about them, not us. I realized that when I coached them. Those games were not about me winning a duel with the other team's coach. They were about teaching kids to be better. Those teams were something they did, not something I did.

Some parents today decide to coach so their child gets to play more. In the end the child does not earn it. This is not good. The parent has done the child no favors; indeed, the parent has associated confusion and unhappiness with sport. This is so because later on the kid will have to make it on his or her own in an environment in which the rules have changed considerably. You should coach because you want to help kids and you recognize athletics are an important element in preparing them to become better people and citizens. And sure, into all of this can be woven a healthy focus on winning. But it is always about the kids, never about you.

In some ways, parents today approach sports like a business plan. They decide if their child is good or not. If the kid shows skills, they end up focusing on just that sport. That can drive the passion right out of the game.

This business mentality has also changed the way kids see athletes. My heroes, above all, were my parents. When I was a kid I looked up to sports stars, too. In baseball season, my hero was Carlton Fisk. During hockey season, it was Bobby Orr. During basketball, it was John Havlicek. For me, each hero I had was in something I was passionate about at the time.

When I was a kid, I watched football. Joe Namath would lead the Jets down the field. Afterward, I would go out in the driveway and pretend I was behind the center. Like I said, one of the greatest things about being on that 1980 Winter Olympic team is that I hear the stories of people who say they pretended to be me in their backyard. Hopefully it was as positive for them as playing Joe Namath was for me. Our team has done a lot to keep that going, but in today's world, that can be a challenge.

Now I think that heroes and role models have more to do with money than passion. It is about how much a person is on television. Kids are looking at stuff like MTV's *Cribs* to determine who they want to be when they grow up. Not only does that sap the passion out of sports, it also sets

Love your kids, and listen to them. They will tell you what they want to do. Once they do, support them but let them shine on their own. It is their time; it will be their memories.

up these kids for unrealistic expectations. It is a recipe for disaster.

When it comes to sports, or anything really, I would give a parent this advice. Love your kids, and listen to them. They will tell you what they want to do. Once they do, support them but let them shine on their own. It is their time; it will be their memories.

I learned this when my kids were young. Now they are grown up. An interesting thing happens as your kids get older. If you have done it right and committed the time and energy and sacrifice to them when they were young, that relationship changes over time. You end up becoming their friend. Experiencing that now, I can tell you that there is no better reward.

One of the biggest challenges faced by parents today is the "two-job lifestyle." I call it that because for some families, having both parents work is a necessity. The kids might not eat without the additional income. To me, that is different. When I say the two-job lifestyle, I am referring to those parents who both work so they can have the materialistic things that they want. For them, there always seems to be a reason that they cannot be home with their kids. To me, that makes no sense. When you decide to have a child, you make a personal sacrifice, just like my parents did. They understood that, and that is why I took the time to find my dad up in the stands that day in February 1980. It is as simple as that.

Cal Ripken Jr. | Family Moments

Cal Ripken Jr. is known as the "Iron Man" of baseball. While playing shortstop and third base with the Baltimore Orioles, he broke a longstanding major league record by playing in 2,632 consecutive games. A 19-time All-Star, he was inducted into the National Baseball Hall of Fame on the first ballot. In 1987, he and his brother Billy Ripken both played infield on the Orioles team managed by their father Cal Ripken Sr. Cal Jr. is the father of a daughter and a son.

I have no doubt I learned so much about being a father from my dad. He taught me the importance of hard work and how to lead by example. His lessons shaped me as a ballplayer and gave me an approach and a work ethic that for sure played a role in the streak. More important, I hope I have passed down his lessons to my kids, so they can pass them down to their own. Family moments are something I value, and they can be fleeting. I learned that in 1987.

The 1987 season is one I will never forget. Although my father was a coach on the Orioles' staff in 1982 when I broke into the majors, he became the manager in 1986. It was July 11, 1987, that stands out to me. It was the day that my brother Bill made his big-league debut as an Oriole. On that day, my father became the first person to ever manage two of his sons at the same time. Together with Billy and my dad, I was doing what I loved. It could not get any better than that.

Unfortunately, our time together ended all too soon. My dad was fired six games into the 1988 season. In total, my dad spent 36 years with the Baltimore Orioles organization. My brother played with me on the Orioles until 1993. But the three of us only had that one season together. It's no wonder that it felt too short.

Not everyone gets to experience a moment like that. I am thankful we had a full season together because although baseball honored me with a great life, family is what really matters. Combining the two is a blessing. Finding the balance between the two—family and work—is more often a challenge.

Time can often get in the way of family. We get busy, and it just slips by. That is one of the greatest challenges when it comes to parenting and why we cannot just do the convenient thing. You have to put in the

Cal Ripken Sr. and family

time to figure out what you want your kids to be exposed to. Learn about them, and be open to their interests. Then be strategic, and get them out there doing it.

Just like parenting, life is about hard work. Sometimes the reward for that work might not be apparent right away. Sometimes you might need something more to motivate you to go that extra mile as a parent. For me, it was about the lessons I learned as a kid, and I learned a lot of those lessons from my dad.

When I was young, our life was a little nomadic. My dad was coaching in the minor leagues, so he wasn't home a lot and we didn't have a lot of money. He would go to work, come home for dinner, and fall down on the couch exhausted. And in the off-season he had part-time jobs.

Dad had so much responsibility when he was managing back then. He had no assistant coaches and did everything himself: charts, pitching batting practice, working out the bullpen, everything. He was very organized, and he had a great system. He had to be, considering the volume of work.

One of the best things about my dad's time managing is that he brought me with him to practices a lot. But there were only small pockets of time I had to interact with him while he was working. A lot of the time I was interacting with the other players. This had an impact on me as a ballplayer.

Dad didn't push me to play baseball. His philosophy was to never push anything on us. He exposed us to opportunities and encouraged us to seek out the things we wanted to do. It was easy for me to love baseball. I was good at it, and I was always hanging around the field with my dad. Everyone was envious that I got to be around professional players, not to mention the fact that I had a dad we used to call "the encyclopedia of baseball."

When I think back and try to see my dad like I did when I was young, I think of him as perfect. When I grew up, I realized his history. He was a jack of all trades because he lost his dad and had to work at an early age. He had to become the man of the house. When I was young, though, I thought he could do everything—fix the lawnmower and the car, plant and build things. He controlled every situation, and I was in awe of him. I really wanted to do something to make him proud. He was my role model, my hero.

Understandably, my dad taught me the importance of hard work. I watched him put in all those hours as a coach, and I saw him come home exhausted. I admired how he took care of things around the house and how he seemed

Baseball's Ripkens (from left): Cal Sr., Billy, and Cal Jr.

like he could do anything. I can trace a lot of my success back to the example he set.

I doubt he led his life the way he did solely to teach me a lesson. If it had all been for show, we probably wouldn't have learned what we did. The reason we learned it was because the lesson was not taught just through words—it was taught through his actions. That's how kids learn; they watch their parents. They learn from them.

Growing up with a father who was a minor league coach had its ups and downs. During the season we would drive to wherever he was. There were four of us, three boys and a girl—I was the second oldest. We relied on each other, playing card games in laundromats and inventing games we could play in motel hallways. There would be athletic games when we had the chance, and any variation of baseball we could come up with. One of our favorites was using one of those small souvenir bats and a Ping-Pong ball. For kids, though, some of the best stuff comes from creativity. The pots and pans in the kitchen used to be a lot of fun, and everyone knows how much kids love a huge cardboard box.

We were very active kids, like our parents. They were both athletes. They were doers and enjoyed sports. We had just enough people to string a volleyball net across the driveway and choose up sides. With the boys, we had so much energy we needed to be outside. The worst times would be when it rained and we were confined to a small space. We were always out on our own, riding bikes around the neighborhood and looking for pickup games.

Because Dad had to travel a lot, when he was home, we competed for his attention. Early on, Dad did three free baseball clinics every Saturday morning for the small town in which he managed. He would come tap me on the knee at 7:00 in the morning.

"You want to come with me?" he'd ask.

It was early and I didn't really want to go listen to someone talk about baseball all morning. I went, though, because I wanted to spend time with Dad in the car. My other siblings didn't want to go, so it would be my private time with him.

This shaped me as a father. I tried to be there even more than my dad could be. It started right at the beginning. When Rachel was born, I had a unique opportunity that most dads don't get. It was the off-season, so I stayed in the room with my wife Kelly and I was the first to change Rachel's diaper. It was special. I think that beginnings are important. They set the tone.

I thought back to that when I retired from baseball. I considered taking a coaching job, but that would be the same schedule I had as a player. It didn't give me much flexibility. By foregoing that, I got to spend time with my kids while they were still living at home. I'd never trade that.

I made a commitment. When I was home I took them to school. I loved that time. It reminded me of driving to the clinics with my dad. I still take my son in, and he's nearing the end of high school. I can close my eyes and picture my daughter's first day of school in 1995. It was the same day that I set the consecutive games record, and it was special

I made a commitment. When I was home I took them to school. I loved that time. It reminded me of driving to the clinics with my dad.

to bring her to school that morning because she was so excited. It is such a wonderful memory to have.

It reminds me of the countless little memories I have of spending time with my dad when I was young. At the age of 10 I'd go to the ballpark, and my dad had established a rule that you couldn't be on the field without wearing a uniform. So they had a little uniform made for me. I'd be out in the field shagging fly balls.

"Go shag in the outfield," Dad instructed me. "Stay out of the way of the other players. If it comes your way, let it hit the fence and throw it in. Never, ever come into the infield—it is too dangerous."

As ironic as it sounds considering how many hours I've clocked in the infield since, those kinds of moments are the ones that stick out. At the time, it was just Dad spending time with me. He was always the professional that way. When Bill and I got drafted, Dad downplayed it. Maybe he wanted to alleviate the pressure on us. Maybe he wanted to make sure that no one thought we were getting special treatment. We had to earn our way like everyone else.

When the media would ask him about us, he'd say, "I was a minor league manager, and I look at all these guys as my sons in a way."

In some ways we wanted to scream and jump up and down and say, "No, we're your *real* sons!"

Instead we went about our business and didn't make a big deal out of it, and we understood what he meant. When Dad got the manager's job, as brief as it was, and Bill got called up, it was really special. I don't think I fully appreciated how special it was until it was over. I had a dad

Cal Ripken Jr. and Sr.

in the locker room. I could go to him for anything. I had a brother to go to for the things that might be tough to take to Dad. Looking back, it was about as good as it could be. The only things that could have been better were having a good team and it could have lasted longer.

Like I said, family is the ultimate priority in life. When I think about which is more challenging, playing so many games without missing one or being a dad, it doesn't take me long to respond. No doubt, the answer is being a dad. Being a parent can be challenging and rewarding. Your kids totally depend on you as you grow them and shape them. It is an around-the-clock responsibility. As parents, if we look at it that way, everything else becomes a little easier.

> *It is an around-the-clock responsibility. As parents, if we look at it that way, everything else becomes a little easier.*

When it comes to teaching them, it boils down to one thing—kids learn from the actions of adults. Work ethic comes from the examples right in front of you. There is a right way and a wrong way of doing things. As Dad used to say, if it is worth doing, it is worth doing right.

Words may fill in the hole every once and a while, but it is all about actions. Kids learn from what you do, and one of the best opportunities to teach them is to get down on the ground and be active with them. Get off the couch and play ball. Learn to ski. Whatever it is that your kids are into, do it. When it is all said and done, you will be so glad you did, and you won't trade that time for the world.

Watching my father, I learned the fundamentals I would need to be the ballplayer I was. That wasn't it, though. I also learned how to be the parent I wanted to be. I wanted kids with a strong work ethic, kids who treated people right, and kids who were active. I did my part to teach them those things. But I know deep down that they learned a lot more from how I acted than what I said. That is one of the reasons I am so proud of my career. Sure, it felt good to be recognized. But it feels even better to show my kids that with hard work, anything is possible.

When I think about playing with my dad when I was a kid, it is easy to see how different times were then. He was a grown-up. He had responsibilities. He had to provide for his family, but he was following his dream at the same time. That had a profound effect on me. Dad used to say that there are too many people in this world doing things that they hate. He and Mom encouraged us to find what we love and pursue it.

> *Dad used to say that there are too many people in this world doing things that they hate. He and Mom encouraged us to find what we love and pursue it.*

In many ways, he was like a little kid, too. When he'd play with us, he would get into the spirit of the game, whether it was Lincoln Logs or baseball. He loved train sets. He was meticulous and a great teacher. When he'd get under the blankets of a fort with us, when he was in the smallest space, he'd almost morph into a kid and do whatever we were doing. In so many cases, he was the most grown-up person I knew. Other times, though, he came down to where we were. He immersed himself in what we were doing.

Like Dad, I tried to be very hands-on as a father, getting down on my knees and immersing myself in whatever they were doing. I still remember the good times. I think about huge leaf piles in the front yard. I can still picture the kids playing in the leaves and throwing them around. We loved big snowstorms. My dad used to make huge piles of snow and dig tunnels out for us. Later, I did the same thing for my kids.

When it comes to parenting, I also learned patience and understanding from my dad. Kids make mistakes. It is part of growing up. He taught us to take responsibility for our mistakes. When I did something wrong, he handled it like he handled life. He might wake me up early and say he needed help gardening. We'd work in silence for the first hour. Then he'd bring it up.

"You had trouble coming home late," he might say.

He wouldn't overreact. He'd hear me out. At the same time, he took care of business and kept us in line. It wasn't hard, though, because we saw him toe the line every day. He led through actions. He had a principled approach to life. He was a doer. He didn't sit around and think about ideas. If we wanted to play soccer, he'd say, "Let's make a field. Let's build the goal." And he'd execute it.

There is no doubt that so much has changed since I was young. I think things are a lot more complicated now. Safety is more of an issue. That's why organized sports start so young. Kids don't have the freedom that we did when we were young. At the same time there are a lot more options on how you interact with your dad. You can wrestle, you can do something physical, or you can play a video game.

There is a trap to video games, though. So many kids have become obsessed with them. They get locked into their own little world. When Ryan was young, he'd ask me to play a game with him. I'd say, "Dad likes the real game. Let's play baseball instead of the MLB video game." My technique relied on his valuing time with me. I would suggest climbing a tree or doing something outside. I always tried to associate activity with doing things with me.

My technique relied on his valuing time with me. I would suggest climbing a tree or doing something outside. I always tried to associate activity with doing things with me.

It is funny. When we were kids, we played a ton of board games and cards. I guess you could say that video games are just board games getting better. I think it is different, though. There is a normal interaction through card games and board games that you don't get through electronics. Let me stress that my kids, like most kids, love video games—and I have no problems with most of them. I just want my kids to achieve a balance, not spend all day on the computer or in front of the TV.

It makes me think about skiing. I never learned how. Once I started playing baseball, it was an occupational hazard. When I was 41, though, I took lessons. It was something I could do with the kids. It was such a great way to share an experience with them.

My 1987 season is a great story. It is unique that my father, brother, and I got to spend a season on the same MLB team, but the reality of a family spending time together should not be. Every family should do that. Life is full of serious lessons. We have to teach our children how to work hard and how to be the best. Every action they see in us becomes a factor in how they will lead their lives in the future. It is an awesome responsibility. At the same time it is an incredible gift. Learn what they like, and be strategic about getting them exposed to it. Be active, lead by example, and be a grown-up—but play with them like a kid.

Like the time Bill and I had with our dad, moments you share with family will fill you with memories that you will carry throughout life. And it will fill your children with the lessons they need to succeed and lead healthy, active lives. At the same time, you'll be teaching your kids to be great parents, and everything will come full circle.

Nolan Ryan | The Family Express

Nolan Ryan is a former Major League Baseball player. He played an amazing 27 years with the New York Mets, California Angels, Houston Astros, and Texas Rangers. He was inducted into the National Baseball Hall of Fame in 1999. He pitched a record-setting seven no-hitters during his career and regularly threw the ball more than 100 mph. He is the father of three.

As far back as I can remember, I was always throwing something. Early on, it was rocks or things of that nature. Later on, although it may sound corny, it was newspapers. From the second grade until I graduated from high school, I was rolling and throwing papers. Much of that was tossing them out the window with my left hand, however, so I don't believe that had a bearing on my pitching arm.

I grew up very close to my dad. We worked together almost every night. My dad worked two jobs. He was up at 7:00 and home at 4:30. He would go to bed at 8:00 and wake up at 1:00 AM to deliver papers. Then he was back in

Nolan Ryan (left), grandson Jackson, and son Reid

bed at 4:30. He did that so my mother could stay at home with us.

He and my mother made sure that their children had a better life. They were dedicated and committed to their family. I saw all the work that went into that commitment. I saw what it took to keep up with the clothes and activities of my four sisters. I saw the sacrifices my parents made in their lives for their family. It instilled something in me.

I definitely got my work ethic from my parents. I am very appreciative of that. I grew up in an era when we worked and understood the value of work. Even in the summer I had jobs painting houses or mowing lawns. I understood the value of money and I liked having it.

I was the last of six kids for my parents. My dad was 42 when I was born. Having older brothers definitely influenced my athletic development. One of my brothers was seven years older. He played all the sports. When you grew up in Texas at that time, you played whatever was in season. So I tended to tag along with my brother and his buddies, always hoping they needed someone to fill in. That's where my interest in sports developed. At the same time, my parents were very supportive of whatever I pursued. For me it was sports, but for my sisters it was band and piano. They simply encouraged us.

In most ways, I lived the very typical small-town lifestyle of that age. We were outside all the time in the summer. One of the reasons we stayed so active was that we had no air conditioning. When that Texas summer rolled in, Mother wanted you out of the house. It was not as if there was much in the house to begin with. There were no television programs for kids in those days. It was not as if we would stay inside to read a book. That left riding bikes, fishing down on the bayou, and most of all, playing baseball.

One of the reasons we stayed so active was that we had no air conditioning. When that Texas summer rolled in, Mother wanted you out of the house.

We lived in a new neighborhood. There were still many vacant lots for sale. Each summer, we would go to work on one of them. We'd mow the grass and build a backstop. We'd lay out the bases and have a diamond on the vacant field. No one said anything, and we never asked for permission. The neighborhood probably liked it. We kept the grass cut short. By the next summer, that lot might have sold. There might be a house sitting where our field had been. So we would go back to work, starting the entire process anew.

It is no wonder baseball held a special place in my heart. I remember how meaningful it was when my dad purchased my first glove. Remember, I was the last of six kids. Most of what I owned came secondhand. When I was seven or eight, my dad walked me down to the hardware store. At

Two generations of Ryan men

that time, they were transitioning toward the more modern gloves they use today versus the old Hank Greenberg kind with the soft leather and separated fingers. I chose one of those old-fashioned ones. I wanted to be like all those guys I saw on the baseball cards.

I can recall using that glove with pride when I played Little League. That was when I pitched my first no-hitter. In fact, it was a double no-hitter; neither team got a hit that day. The pitcher I faced hit one of our batters, allowing a run in, so we beat them 1–0. I would not pitch another no-hitter until my senior year in high school. Then in the majors, my first came when I was with the Kansas City Royals. My most meaningful one was my seventh. It came late in my career, and even better, it came in Texas, my home. That meant so much to me.

It is funny to think back to the reputation I had as a player. I know batters I faced thought I was mean.

> I was a disciplinarian with my kids. I set high standards. I think my kids would see it that way, but I can remember taking them over to their grandmother's. I marveled—was this the same lady who raised me? I find that now I am the same way with my grandkids.

My relationship to the opposition was that I didn't want to get to know them. I had to be aggressive to win. If I could intimidate, that is what I had to do. I figure there were two Nolans—normal Nolan and competitive Nolan. I wanted the opposition to know I would do anything to help my team win.

I never brought that home. The kids never really knew competitive Nolan, at least not in the way big-league hitters did. I was a disciplinarian with my kids. I set high standards. I think my kids would see it that way, but I can remember taking them over to their grandmother's. I marveled—was this the same lady who raised me? I find that now I am the same way with my grandkids.

Sometimes when I think back to my upbringing, I cannot help but compare it to my children's. I grew up in a community of maybe 5,000 to 7,000 people. I might have left the state of Texas twice. My world was very small, pretty much focusing on activities in Alvin and stuff at school.

My kids grew up traveling around the country. They are more well-rounded than I was, and most of that was due to baseball. When I went to Houston as a free agent, my son Reid was in first grade. The kids were still young and would go on road trips with me. My career became incorporated into the family. For us, it was important that we were together.

Even if they stayed behind, I made it a point to focus on them when I got home. When I was with the California Angels, I remember flying home from Boston. We got back around 5:00 or 6:00 AM. The kids got me out of bed at 8:00 because they wanted to play ball in the backyard. At the time, it was hard. Now I am reaping the rewards.

I can recall one spring training when we took them out of school. We got all of the work they needed to do from their school. We got together with Phil Garner and some others and put together a classroom for the kids. We hired a substitute teacher, and the kids would go to school. They did their lesson plan, and by the time they got back from spring training, they weren't behind at all. When they were done working, and in between games, we would go out onto the field. I would hit balls to them or pitch to them in the cage. They were around baseball so often, it is natural that they gravitated toward the sport.

Today, I doubt that you could get approval to do something like that. Back then, the laws were different. By the 1990s, I remember the kids coming down sporadically during the spring. I missed those times that we could all be together.

When they were not in school, they continued to go on road trips with me. The boys got the chance to be our batboy and just be around the park. It taught them how to travel and gave them the chance to be around people. All in all, it was a very good education. Ruth and Wendy also traveled when they could. Those were great times being all together like that.

Obviously different people have different attitudes toward life. For us, family was important. Just because I lived the life of a baseball player didn't mean we couldn't be together. It was an opportunity to bring experiences and education to our children through travel and through the game. That was an

Just because I lived the life of a baseball player didn't mean we couldn't be together. It was an opportunity to bring experiences and education to our children through travel and through the game.

opportunity not too many people got to have. Considering I was away from home 15 days a month, it was very important to me, too.

My kids were raised in a different time. I wanted them to have the opportunity to be kids. My wife Ruth and I were both sports-minded. We wanted the kids to enjoy sports, and we supported that to the fullest. I was blessed that my kids were athletic and enjoyed sports. Now that tradition has passed on to another generation. Just the other Saturday, I went to three basketball games for the church league. I was a proud grandfather.

I cannot take all of the credit. A good bit has to go to Ruth. She and I grew up together in Alvin. We've known each other since we were around 10 years old. We got married when I was 20 and she was 18. A lot of our success may be attributed to the fact that we came from similar upbringings. She has a close relationship with her family, even though they are scattered all over the country.

As a mother, she was very involved. She loved the kids' activities, and she was very active with their school. We were blessed that she could be a stay-at-home mother. Today in our society, that family unit is more challenged than ever before. Mothers have to leave the home for employment. There are other people raising our children. I am fortunate that my two daughters-in-law and my daughter do not have to work. They stay at home and raise their kids as we did and as my mother did for us. It is unfortunate so many mothers do not have that opportunity. I think that can lead to a lot of disconnect in a family.

When you become a parent, I think you have a responsibility and obligation. On a personal basis, you can really miss a lot. Time goes by so quickly with your children. The last thing you want to do is have regrets. You never want to look back and feel like you didn't develop the relationship you needed to with your kids.

> *Time goes by so quickly with your children. The last thing you want to do is have regrets.*

Today I talk to my kids practically every day. We are involved in business ventures together. They run some of our businesses. To have that kind of relationship with grown children it depends on the attitude and commitment you showed your family when they were young. Now I see my kids and my grandkids a lot. Even with my job with the Rangers, I make sure I get home for the important things. My attitude has not changed over time. In the end it is simple, but it might not be convenient. You get out of it what you put in.

It is hard to speculate what my relationships would be like now if I had not put in the time earlier. I know it could not be as close as it is today. I feel for people whose children are scattered all over the country. It can happen considering employment and marriage. Many grandparents have little access to their grandkids except for special occasions. I feel very fortunate that I have all my children and grandchildren here in Texas with me.

The interesting thing about parenthood is the impact it has on your life. I do not think anyone who hasn't experienced it can understand just how profound it is. On the day my kids were born, my life definitely changed. I hope every new parent out there embraces that change. Parenthood is the greatest thing that can happen to you.

Mike Eruzione | Seize Those Moments

Mike Eruzione is a former Olympic hockey player. He was the captain of the 1980 U.S. Olympics men's hockey team that beat the Soviets in a game known as the "Miracle on Ice," and he scored the winning goal of that game. He is the father of three.

Life is a series of moments. Each moment presents us with a new opportunity. So many of those moments pass without us seizing the potential they represent. I hear all the time from people who have regrets or from people who look back and wish they had done this or that when they had the chance. I always tell them one thing—it is not too late.

When the 1980 U.S. hockey team took the ice against the Soviet Union, we were not given a chance to win. They had crushed the teams they faced before us. They were the juggernaut of hockey, having won every gold medal since 1964, and we were just the boys from the USA.

Hovering over that game was something even bigger. Things were tough. The United States economy was down.

The Eruzione family

The Soviets had invaded Afghanistan, and 53 Americans were being held hostage in Iran. The Cold War was hitting its peak. When we met the Soviets in a medal-round game, there was no way that it would stay "just a hockey game." Not in that climate.

Although the Soviets jumped out to an early 1–0 lead, we stuck with them. By the end of the first period, it was tied 2–2. The Soviets scored in the second period to take the lead. In the third, my teammate Mark Johnson tied it up. Then, while skating down the ice, the puck came to me. I fired a shot past the right arm of the Soviet goalkeeper. We took the lead with only 10 minutes left to play. That goal sealed the victory now known as the "Miracle on Ice."

Today, I travel all over the country speaking to audiences. I often show that 4-minute video. To get a laugh, I say it is my life story. My friend jokes with me that if the puck had gone 2 inches to the left, I would be painting bridges instead of giving speeches. That's what I did in college to earn money. I laugh and tell him that it didn't go 2 inches to the left; it went right where it was supposed to go. The video goes over well with audiences, but we all know that there is more to life than just 4 minutes.

I believe that life is really about the time you spend with your kids. Every one of those minutes count. In today's world, that time is even more important. So much has changed. Kids stay inside now, watching TV or playing video games. When was the last time you saw a pick-up game in the empty lot down the street? When was the last time you had to stop your car because kids were playing ball in the street? Now the responsibility to keep kids active falls directly on the parents' shoulders. If we fail them, our kids won't be ready to seize their opportunity, score their goals, and make the most of their lives.

It is not a one-time thing, though. It takes commitment. As a parent, even when you are tired, you have to get up and get your kids active in something that they love. It can't be done once and forgotten. It takes way more than 1 minute. That is the hard part.

> *The responsibility to keep kids active falls directly on the parents' shoulders. If we fail them, our kids won't be ready to seize their opportunity, score their goals, and make the most of their life.*

For me, it is easy to think of life as a few minutes of time that stand out. My entire hockey career came down to 4 minutes and one opportunity that I seized. Had it played out any differently, who knows how my life would have unfolded?

I can even trace when I started playing hockey back to one game. I didn't start to take part in organized hockey until I was 12. That's not to say that some of my fondest childhood memories didn't involve hockey. I remember calling up friends and saying, "Let's go down to the tennis courts." We'd end up with 20 guys down there. In the winter we might flood the court, or we'd go to the swamp when it froze. It was always fun, but there was no structure. We'd just meet at 7:00 in the morning and play.

When I got ready for college, though, I thought my short hockey career might come to an end. My plan was to go to the University of New Hampshire, but the hockey coach there said I wasn't good enough. I ended up deciding to play hockey for Merrimac, a Division II school.

One day, during the summer before my freshman year, a friend told me about a summer hockey game. He was looking for someone to play. I hadn't shot a puck in a while, but I agreed to go along with him. It ended up that Jack Parker, who at the time was the assistant coach at Boston University, was refereeing the game. I played well, and afterward he asked me where I was going to school. I told him Merrimac. He told me that a kid he had recruited from Canada had decided not to come to BU and play. He said he had a spot open.

There was no way my parents could afford to send me to Boston University. I told him so, and he offered me a full scholarship. Just like that, my hockey career was back on and better than I could have imagined. In one moment, the opportunity jumped right out at me.

I was lucky because it was hard to miss that one. There was no way I would say no. But if you look deeper into it, you can see that moment may not have come about at all. Having been disappointed by not getting the chance to play in college, I could have turned down the chance to play. Even after I agreed to go along with my friend, I could have half-assed it on the ice. At the time I wasn't playing for anything but the love of the game, but I went out there and gave it my all. Thank God I did.

What set me up to succeed at that one moment in time? What in my life prepared me to seize that opportunity? I think I would have to say it was my childhood. It was the time I spent with my family.

Not too many people grow up the way I did. I wish they could. I grew up in Winthrop, Massachusetts. We lived in a three-family house. My mother's brother lived upstairs. He married my father's sister, and they had five kids. My father's sister lived downstairs with her husband and three kids. In all, 14 cousins lived in the same house, including me.

My cousin Tony was in the lead. He got us playing every day. We'd start up a game of stickball, half ball, or curtain rod hockey—whatever he suggested. We'd play in the kitchen or in the garage. We even constructed a hockey arena outside. Cousin Tony lined the rink with storm windows so we could check into the glass. Once I checked Tony through the glass. It was a lucky shot; he was a little older than I was. My aunt flipped out.

We were always in the backyard, and we didn't need all the best toys to have a good time. Sometimes we'd take the broken half of a wooden bat and use that to hit baby building blocks across the yard. Whatever was on the schedule, it started first thing in the morning. We'd march out of the house, only returning for a quick lunch, and then we came in after hearing our parents' shouts for dinner as the sun was setting.

In a house like that, you can just imagine what Christmas was like. After opening our presents, we rushed around to see what everyone else got. It is a wonder the house didn't fall down with all those kids stomping up and down the stairs. In the end, 90 percent of the gifts were sports-related.

We were definitely into sports. The entire family was very competitive. When we got together, we'd head to the park for a picnic. We had enough to field a great softball game. My dad played catcher. In fact, he caught fast-pitch softball for thirty years.

The adults would play hockey, too. I remember my father and uncle getting out there. My dad was busy a lot of the time. He worked three jobs, and he couldn't skate. But he would get in the goal wearing his boots. He, along with my uncle, always made time for baseball. They used to grab a bat and a ball and hit us grounders.

For Dad, it wasn't all about being the best athlete. When I played hockey, he came to the games but he wouldn't sit with my mom. She sat with a friend, and my dad would go higher up in the stands. He didn't like people to see him react. During one game I scored five goals. On the fifth, he jumped into the air and fell back four rows. He thought no one saw him.

He got into the games in a good way. He would say, "Way to go, Big Mike." He'd never say anything when I played poorly. I don't think he cared how well I played. With him, it was about how hard I played. If I fumbled or struck out, it didn't matter as long as I tried my hardest. There was no jogging to first base with him. I would say that was the kind of stuff that prepared me for that moment in time when I got my big break.

With all that play, it's not surprising that we ended up athletes. All five of the boy cousins played three sports in school. For me, it was football, hockey, and baseball. Cousin Tony went on to play football at Xavier. He was actually in the game highlighted in the movie *We Are Marshall*. All that playing connected us to the community in a way only sports and family can.

It is no wonder that I still live in the same neighborhood. From my backyard I can see the old house. My father lives there to this day with his two sisters and my mother's brother. Cousin Tony built a house in that backyard we used to play in. He coaches football in town. Not long ago, the new gang of cousins hit the scene. For the high school baseball team, my son batted first, his brother second, and his cousins third, fifth, and seventh.

No doubt because of how I grew up, I consider time with my kids to be priceless. I like to be involved in their sports. I coached both of my sons, more so with my younger one.

No doubt because of how I grew up, I consider time with my kids to be priceless.

I was usually an assistant coach for hockey.

A good amount of the time I spend with them focuses on athletics. Once when my son Michael was five, I took him to the high school gym to fool around. Street hockey nets were set up. Michael really wanted to play goalie. At first I didn't want him to, but he kept at me. Finally I said okay.

With my five-year-old in the net, I tried to be careful. I went to shoot one over his shoulder and instead hit him square on the forehead. It was a hard one. He started walking toward me from the net. He looked dazed and said, "Me no be goalie no more."

I know that life can sometimes get in the way. There were times when my work kept me away, but I always hated missing my kids' games. One time I was in Puerto Rico when my youngest was playing baseball. I called right after the game, and my wife told me he had hit one over the fence. I knew the fence she was talking about. It measured about 500 feet. He was only the second kid ever to have done that. My whole family had been there. I felt sick. That's when I realized there was no amount of money in the world that was worth missing that home run.

That is why I even go to their practices when I am home. When I was in sports, parents never went to practice. But for my kids' teams, there were 15 to 20 parents there. I knew I was going to be away for a week, so I wanted to be there. It was fun for me.

Fortunately, my kids were pretty good in sports. But that shouldn't matter. I think back to my dad. He never cared if we were the best. He expected me to work hard. That is what I expect from my kids. One of my daughters is not as athletic, but she did gymnastics. In eighth grade she ran track. During a hurdles event, a girl from the other team fell down, and my daughter stopped to help her up. I smiled. I knew she was doing the best she could, and I loved to see that kindness inside her.

Not every kid is going to love every sport. Some may not like any sports. That is okay, too. The one rule I had with my kids was that they were going to do something. They were going to be active. They were not going to sit and watch television or play video games.

> Not every kid is going to love every sport. Some may not like any sports. That is okay, too. The one rule I had with my kids was that they were going to do something. They were going to be active.

It is the challenge all parents face today. The world has changed. I look around at kids today, and I am amazed at how many have never skated on ice outside. Even my kids, who played hockey, haven't. I call them "refrigerator kids" because we were always looking at the refrigerator to see what was next on their schedule. Nothing was in the spur of the moment.

In my day, parents kicked their kids out of the house. Now there are a lot of single parents. People don't want to leave their kids at the playground because they don't know who is out there. Maybe it is a safety issue. Maybe it is just the new reality that kids have to be scheduled and that their activity has to be organized. Because of that, though, parents have to take a far more involved role in making sure the kids are active.

Some parents might think that if their kids don't like sports, there is nothing else they can do. There is, though. Take them bowling instead. Put your kids in a position to try new things. Go hiking or take them to the pool for a swim. Take them skiing or even to a museum and walk around all day. There are a lot of things out there now. Anything is better than letting them stay in the house all day.

If you don't, the consequences are easy to see. Kids are overweight. They don't do anything. They don't eat right. There are a ton of things to do out there. As a parent, you have to find them. If you say you don't have the time, shame on you. You have to find it. To me, it is as important as finding the time to get your kids to the doctor if they are sick.

The way that sports, and life for that matter, have changed for kids is not healthy. It is very unfortunate to see a fourth grader who is 100 pounds overweight. Some schools have taken physical education out of the curriculum. Kids are not learning how to exercise. You can have a brilliant mind, but if you are morbidly obese and die in your twenties, what good is it? The mind and the body and the soul all work together. Without one, the others can't reach their full potential.

So what do you do? I think kids need to learn how to adapt to this new world by example. I think it is great for kids who are playing a sport to look up to professionals as inspiration. Today, though, I see kids looking up to athletes like they are heroes. Some of those athletes are great. Some are not so great.

I have to admit that when I hear people like Pat LaFontaine or Jeremy Roenick asked about how they got into hockey and they answer that they pretended to be Mike Eruzione in the basement as a kid, it touches me. I think the 1980s Olympic team may have opened the door for American players to get into the NHL. Now that door has been blown down, but in my time, the league didn't consider Americans too often. We may have started it, but guys like Brian Leetch and Keith Tkachuk brought it to a whole new level.

Either way, I think it is too easy for athletes today. I think Charles Barkley was right in his Nike ad. He could have said it differently, but his point was valid. These kids should be looking up to teachers, parents, or soldiers. Those are the role models and heroes of life. I remember looking up to Bill Russell as a kid, but I didn't know him. My role models were my parents and my coaches.

In reality, my miracles are my children, seeing them born and watching them grow. It is harder to be a parent than a captain of the Olympic hockey team. As captain, I was surrounded by great people. As a parent, you might be forced to be around people with whom you don't want to associate—be it a difficult parent or a kid who isn't the best influence on yours.

As a parent, though, it is no different than anything else. Life is a series of moments, and all of them are opportunities to help your kids grow up healthy and happy. Anyone who has a child knows just how fast time passes. Before long, you turn around and your kids are grown up and moving on. When that happens, the one thing you do not want to do is to be left looking back at all those moments that passed and all those opportunities that were missed.

These kids should be looking up to teachers, parents, or soldiers. Those are the role models and heroes of life.

Everyone gets an opportunity. It is what you make of it that matters. I could have gone to that summer game and just gone through the motions. If I had, I never would have played on the Olympic team. Instead, I listened to my dad. I played hard and seized that moment.

Your kids will look to you when their moment comes. It's up to you to start laying the foundation your kids will need to succeed. All it takes is for you to grab that next moment and start down a whole new path, a path which there is no way you will regret.

Bob and Aaron Boone | A Baseball Family

Bob Boone is a former Major League Baseball player. His father played in the majors, as did two of his sons, Bret and Aaron. All four of the Boones were named to an All-Star team during their careers. Currently GM and vice president of player development for the Washington Nationals, Bob is the father of three.

Aaron Boone is a former Major League Baseball player. He is known for hitting the eleventh-inning home run for the Yankees during Game 7 of the 2003 American League Championship Series. That hit sent the Yankees to the World Series and continued the Boston Red Sox's "Curse of the Bambino." He is an analyst for ESPN's Baseball Tonight.

With three generations of Boones to have gone through the major-league ranks, the Boones are arguably base-ball's most famous family. Bob and his son Aaron shared their experiences of growing up around the game.

Bob Boone: Ray Boone was an All-Star infielder with the Cleveland Indians, Detroit Tigers, Chicago White Sox, Kansas City Athletics, Milwaukee Braves, and Boston Red Sox. He later became a scout for the Red Sox. He is also my dad.

I was raised exactly the same as I raised my boys. My father was playing Major League Baseball when I was a child. Everything in our lives revolved around the sport. In 1948 he was a rookie with the Cleveland Indians. He was called up in September of that year and went on to win the World Series, although I think he had only one at-bat in the Series. I was there at the time, but I was only 10 months old, so I do not remember it.

I was the oldest. I had a brother who played baseball and a sister who was a wonderful swimmer. We had a fantastic childhood. We were taken out of school for spring training and would have six weeks of school there. We lived in Detroit, but we spent the summers in Cleveland when my dad was with the Indians. Everything in our lives revolved around baseball.

When my kids were young, I went into the army. Bret, my oldest, was one year old at the time. My wife moved in with my parents, so Bret got the chance to live with my father for a while. They forged a special relationship. My dad got him involved in baseball by the time he could walk. Dad was a loving guy and cherished his grandkids.

I was blessed to be born in an athletic family. My uncle, Dr. Brown, is in the College Football Hall of Fame. My cousins were all good athletes. Everything in our life was about sports. It was not just the males of the family. My mom and aunt were great synchronized swimmers. They played every sport in high school. My aunt was a world-class softball pitcher.

Because of that, many of the life lessons I learned from my dad came from sports, particularly baseball. Sometimes it was just about Dad being there with

I was blessed to be born in an athletic family.

me, maybe catching a bullpen session or having a catch in the backyard. He came to my football practices all the time, but it was hard for him to get to my baseball games. By that time he was a scout. Sometimes he would have to be somewhere else in town watching another kid play. Like I said, everything was about baseball.

My dad made me "old school," if there is such a thing. It was all about being tough, although he did not necessarily teach me that. It was just the way we led our lives. It was the way he lived his life. That can be a much more powerful teacher than simply words. I think his lessons were reflected in my 19 years in the majors.

It was really life lessons through baseball. Our conversations would not go much deeper than sports and how to handle certain situations. I remember him talking to me about a situation in Philadelphia. I had been the starter, but after some changes it seemed I was going to be platooning at catcher. Initially, I wanted to be traded. I talked to Dad, and he said, "I'd be damned if I let some guy run me out of town." So I committed to being a better player instead of blaming it on my new competition.

I took his advice when it came to signing my first contract, too. I was not drafted out of high school. I was pretty crushed. My dad had told everyone I was going to college. He sat me down and told me that a team had offered me $35,000 to play. I said, "Hell, yeah." He said, "I told them no, you're going to Stanford."

Ray Boone with sons Bob (center) and Rodney

Another one was when the Phillies asked me to catch. I was resistant. I was drafted as a third baseman and came out of college right into high A. I did pretty well, went to instructional league, and was asked to spring training. Then I had to go into the army for a year. When I came out they asked me to be a catcher. I wanted to be an everyday player, and I thought they would make me a utility player if I switched over to be a catcher. My dad had played catcher, went through the minors as a catcher, then played short-stop for the Indians. That was an unusual move. So I talked to him a lot about the situation.

I told him I didn't want to be a utility player. He left it up to me, but he helped me talk it through. Switching to catcher ended up being the best move of my career.

When I was younger it was not like he taught me how to play baseball. I was just around it every second of my life, much like my sons were. I am sure my first word was probably "ball." I played all three sports, though. So did all three of my sons. My dad did show me the correct swing, and we practiced sliding in the house. I ended up being a pretty good pitcher in high school. I would throw with him, and he would tell me stuff like Bob Lemon said this or Early Wynn—both Hall of Fame pitchers with the Indians—grips it this way.

> *When I was younger it was not like Dad taught me how to play baseball. I was just around it every second of my life, much like my sons were. I am sure my first word was probably "ball."*

Aaron Boone: Ray Boone was my gramps. He was an awesome gramps. He was the patriarch of our baseball family, and he was baseball through and through. I listened to his stories about playing as a little kid. He grew up in San Diego and loved Ted Williams. Williams was every kid's hero. Gramps was a scout until the time he passed away. He knew and loved baseball, and he passed it down to all of us.

BB: The Boones are known as the first three-generation All-Stars in baseball, so I get asked a lot how we did it. The one thing I want parents to have is a concept of making it to the big leagues in baseball, or playing any professional sport. As a kid goes up the food chain in athletics, it gets tougher and tougher at each level. Parents sometimes want it so badly for their children that serious pressure is created.

For us, sports were not meant to be a means toward a great life or a lot of money. They were about enjoying what you were doing. My dad taught me that there are so many life lessons to be learned from sports. They are ingrained in our culture. They teach children how to have fun. Even if a kid strikes out every time he's up, it should not diminish the person he is.

In sports, so few people make it to the professional level. Yet there is so much they can still learn. I think that as a family, if you join a team you honor that commitment. When

> *For us, sports were not meant to be a means toward a great life or a lot of money. They were about enjoying what you were doing.*

you sign up it is like signing a contract that you will be there for the team. It transcends vacation or any other plans.

When you make that commitment, it should be made for the right reason. It should be to have fun. If you want to make it to the next level—at anything really—you'd better be having fun at it or you will get chewed up. It is all about giving it everything you have. So when you are faced with pressure, it should have nothing to do with the big game. It should be your desire to give it all you have and commit to it fully. God tells you whether there is enough ability there to be the best.

With my kids, just like my dad, I never forced them into the game. My job was more to make sure their heads were on straight. Really there was nothing I could do to keep them away from baseball. We were just blessed by our situation. When I was with the Phillies, my boys got to come along with me to work. They would shag balls during batting practice. If I ever left early for the park before they got home, I had hell to pay for it.

It was an amazing upbringing that I was able to give the kids. They learned how to be around the other players. It taught them how to act in a major league setting. For me, it was the same. And it was time to spend with my dad. I am grateful to the Phillies and the Los Angeles Angels for letting me have my kids with me.

AB: Growing up, it was not all baseball. I have great memories of playing horse with my dad and brothers. Dad liked to tell us he was a good basketball player when he was in high school. But that was in the 1960s, the time of set shots. His idea of a trick shot was the running left-handed underhanded scoop in the key.

I remember when I was young I played football in Pop Warner. Dad used to take me to the games on Saturday mornings, he would tape up my ankles. I played running back, but I don't know if I needed my ankles taped. I know I thought it was pretty cool.

That's not to say we didn't spend a ton of time with Dad at the ballfield. If he left before my brothers and I got home from school, we would all be mad at him. We were really fortunate to have a dad who would take us along to his work. Our playground was the major leagues.

Our playground was the major leagues.

It got to the point that we were given our own locker at Vet Stadium. It was the best. Those Phillies teams had some great players. I remember pitcher Tug McGraw teaching Bret to catch flies behind his back. He was magic with a glove at a very young age. It was hard to wrap your brain around. I remember catching my first fly at six years old. It is no wonder we couldn't wait to get to the ballpark.

BB: My boys came to work with me a lot. They, like me, were very exposed to the game. They came to Veterans Stadium and shagged flies in the outfield. They were going in every day, and I am thankful to Danny Ozark, Philadelphia Phillies manager, for allowing it.

Baseball's Boone family

Today you could not do that. It is too big a business, and it would probably be a liability issue. Back then I think it appealed to the fans. They saw the kids out there catching balls. They were young, so it stood out. Also, Tug McGraw had taught Bret how to catch the ball behind his back. Having a 10-year-old kid do that on the warning track was kind of a draw.

Eventually, they were there so much that Kenny Bush, the clubhouse manager, just gave them a locker. Luckily there was space. So they would walk in and get into their uniforms every day. They knew how to be respectful and how to disappear when the tension came, which helped. I loved those times.

I didn't know then that one day I would be able to coach and manage them in the big leagues. I was the bench coach when Bret came to the Cincinnati Reds. I got to manage Aaron there. It was a very special gift. It came with some challenges, as well. As a coach, I tried to treat them like I treated any other player. Once the game started, I watched them as a dad. It was great that I got to see them play all the time.

They handled it great, as well. They knew they could not come up to Dad and ask who was starting or when a certain pitcher was going to be pulled. That was stuff coaches and managers kept to themselves. They understood that, which probably came from the time they spent in the clubhouse at such an early age.

AB: By the time Dad took over in Cincinnati, I was already established there. I was one of the leaders on the team. I knew that there were going to be times when certain guys on the team would end up getting pissed at the manager. I never wanted them to think, "Oh, here comes Aaron, we'd better watch what we say."

Dad really treated me well. Some fathers in that situation might have been harder on their sons. Some might have been too easy. Dad handled it very well. I don't think it was that hard for him because he is just a really good guy. That was the gift he gave me.

When someone asks me if there will be a fourth generation, my wife

> *When someone asks me if there will be a fourth generation, my wife rolls her eyes. My son is going to do whatever he wants to do. I don't have a preference as long as it is something that he loves.*

rolls her eyes. My son is going to do whatever he wants to do. I don't have a preference as long as it is something that he loves. I hope he contributes to society.

Chances are he will have some athletic ability. At four, he's already started baseball classes on Saturdays. They stretch and run the bases. They play catch and hit off the tee. He's picking it up pretty well. I hope he gets something out of it and enjoys his time with baseball. If it ends up being something he is good at, I'll support him. And I will only push him if he needs it.

I was traded to the Yankees to play third base in 2003. I did okay, but I struggled when the Yankees faced the Boston Red Sox in the American League Championship Series. I didn't start Game 7. I came into the game as a pinch runner in the eighth inning during our rally. We were down 5–2, and we tied it up.

The moment was huge. This is before the Red Sox broke the "Curse of the Bambino" and won the World Series in 2004. It was Game 7, the final game of the ALCS. Whoever won was going to the World Series. With the game tied, I was set to lead off the eleventh inning. It might sound cliché, but every kid who has grown up playing Wiffle ball in the backyard imagines that scenario—extra innings, tied game, you are up at the plate, and you hit one over the fence. I am so thankful that I got to experience something like that.

I remember running off the field that inning. I knew I was leading off, and I was thinking, "I am going to do something." I had a good feeling. I remember Joe Torre telling me to stay through the middle. I was going to take a pitch, but then I said, "Screw it. If I get a good pitch, hit it."

I stepped up to the plate with the score tied at 5–5. I knew the pitch was going to be a knuckleball from Tim Wakefield. So I swung, and I hit the ball over the left-field fence. It ended the game. The Yankees moved on, and the Sox went home. It was an incredible moment in my life.

BB: I'll never forget when Aaron hit that home run in the eleventh inning of Game 7 of the 2003 American League Championship Series. It was against the Boston Red Sox, and the hit sent the Yankees to the World Series. I was out hunting elk that day with friends. We came in early enough to see the game. The circumstances leading up to that hit were difficult. I had been fired after the All-Star break. Aaron was struggling with the Yankees. I remember talking to him about just trying to do something to help the team. If he was not hitting, he could make a play with the glove.

We spent so much time together on the field and off. That is what it is all about, really. That is what I think about when I think about the Boones and baseball.

We sat down to a dinner party and to watch the game. When Aaron entered the game in the eighth, I said he would probably hit a home run in the eleventh. Sitting there, it was made even more special by the fact that Bret was in the booth announcing the game. When Aaron hit that ball, his brother went speechless. The moment was special for the whole family. My cell phone rang off the hook. I thought about how my dad had worked for the Red Sox for so many years and the many twists and turns of the game of baseball. That hit went down as one of the biggest plays of the game, but I hope we are known for more than that. For us, sports is about family, and our family is about sports. We spent so much time together on the field and off. That is what it is all about, really. That is what I think about when I think about the Boones and baseball.

Arnold Palmer | Growing Up on the Golf Course

Arnold Palmer is a legendary golfer and golf course designer. He won the Masters four times. He was inducted into the World Golf Hall of Fame in 1974 and won the PGA Tour Lifetime Achievement Award in 1998. He has two daughters and is now a great-grandfather. His grandson, Sam Saunders, is now a professional tournament golfer.

I was born the same year that Wall Street crashed, so I grew up during the heart of the Great Depression. Money was scarce for almost everyone, and jobs were hard to come by. Out of that, I was fortunate to get to spend a great deal of time with my father, Milfred "Deacon" Palmer.

When my sister was born, I was two years old. That's when I started to go to the golf course with my father. He was the course superintendent at Latrobe Country Club near Pittsburgh, Pennsylvania. I spent the day with him and the guys who worked with him. This would go on until I left for college.

When I was with my father, I hung on every word he said. I watched him do his job. He worked hard and did everything precisely. He was in charge of all the equipment on the golf course, kept the fairways perfect, and taught golf to the members.

My time at the golf course included a lot of playing golf. I played some rounds with my father. Whenever he asked, I jumped at the chance. On other days, my sister

Arnold Palmer and grandson Sam Saunders

would caddie for me, or sometimes we would go around the course playing cowboys and Indians. We spent our time doing the things kids do.

Even if it wasn't golfing, I spent a lot of time at the golf course with my father. He taught me how to drive the tractor. He was a strict disciplinarian, but I loved being with him. At the same time, I was scared to death of disappointing him. I remember sitting on his lap as I steered that tractor. It was one of those old Fordson tractors, and it was very tough to steer. I had to stand up to turn the wheel it was so difficult. I was so worried I would put the wheel of the tractor on the side of the hill where it might spin. If I did, he would get on my case. I was always very careful not to do things to disturb him, mostly because I enjoyed being with him so much.

It was not solely on the golf course. My sister and I couldn't wait for Fridays. That was the night my father took us to the movie theater. On Saturday morning my mother would drop me off at the theater and pick me up later in the day.

There were not as many things to do back then as there are now, but we were together as a family all the time. I remember taking skiing trips with my father. He would also make ice skating rinks at the golf course for us. He did all the things you would like to think a father should do. I also played a little golf with him.

When I was four years old, he cut down a set of women's golf clubs for

There were not as many things to do back then as there are now, but we were together as a family all the time.

me. One of the first things he taught me was how to grip the club properly. It was a standard overlapping grip. Pressure in the three fingers of the right hand. Small finger overlapped with the index finger of the left hand. Pressure with the middle two fingers of the left hand. A V between the thumb and index finger between both hands. Pointing to the seam in my shirt on the right shoulder. I have used that grip now for 80 years.

When we played golf together, he would spend the first five minutes talking to me about what I should do. Then we would spend the next three hours together and he would not say a word. That made me want to do better than ever.

> *When we played golf together, he would spend the first five minutes talking to me about what I should do. Then we would spend the next three hours together and he would not say a word.*

His influence was not simply about the game of golf. He taught me to take my hat off when I went inside, and the proper manners when holding a knife and fork. All those things he taught me stayed with me my whole life. I learned how to say "yes, ma'am" and "no, sir." These were the things he thought were important. He felt they would help me in life, and they did. His teachings have meant the world to me as I have grown up.

Everything I did as I grew up I did to impress my father. Whether it was my conduct or my disposition, I wanted to see his reaction to how I did things. It was very, very important to me as a young man.

He was not one to hand out accolades or compliments without a good reason. I worked extremely hard to impress him with everything I did. When it worked, I was very pleased. It meant more because I knew I had earned it when he gave me a compliment.

That went on throughout my life for as long as my father was around. When I won a golf tournament, he would

Sam Saunders and Arnold Palmer circa 1994

congratulate me very softly, then tell me the things I could improve. He always said that telling him something didn't really matter. What mattered was the actions. He wanted me to show him. That's the way it was.

I think we passed on those same lessons to my kids. I definitely used the things my father taught me to help them learn to be proper people. I cannot take all the credit, though. Their mother Winnie raised them extremely well.

Winnie was a very thoughtful person. She cared for her children in a great way. She was very generous and educated our kids above and beyond what they learned in school. She also educated them in personal matters.

I am very pleased and proud of my daughters. They are very nice adults now, and they have lived their lives pretty well. My youngest has four children. Her youngest, Sam Saunders, is a professional golfer playing tournament golf. Two of her three daughters are married and producing great-grandchildren for me. Her other daughter is an engineer in Atlanta. My other daughter, Peggy, has two younger children who are in high school.

One of the things I am most proud of is the way my daughters conduct themselves. They have great manners, and they know all the things my father taught me. They have practiced those lessons in their life and have taught their children in the same way. It is great to see my father's lessons being passed on to yet another generation. I hope to see it passed to my great-grandchildren as well, but they are still very young. I'll be watching.

It is amazing, considering the change in times, that there was not too great a difference between how my daughters were raised and how they raised their children. It is a whole different world today than when I was raised. We gave our kids values I feel are important in life. Not too many people are passing on those same values any longer. Not enough parents are spending the time to teach children manners and educate them on how to conduct themselves.

It is great to see my father's lessons being passed on to yet another generation. I hope to see it passed to my great-grandchildren as well, but they are still very young. I'll be watching.

I feel so fortunate to see my grandchildren grow up with those values, though. I have been blessed to be able to help teach my grandson Sam to golf. I am still teaching him. He is my pupil. He is a very nice 22-year-old. He has good manners. Sam knows I am watching his every step.

With Sam, I think about the time I spent with my father. I do give him compliments, maybe more than my father gave to me, but not overly so. I think it is important that you do that. It worked for me, and I hope it works with Sam.

Helping Sam learn golf is also different than how I learned. He is my grandson, so I do not have as much time with him as I had with my father. He does have a great golf swing and a lot of potential. As he grew up, he caddied for me as well as doing anything he could around the course. Although I wish he had stayed in school and finished his degree at Clemson before going professional, I hope he continues doing what he is doing. Then I will think about forgiving him for dropping out.

In all seriousness, there is something about Sam that I am so proud of. People often come to me and tell me how he does when I am not around. They mention his manners and his courtesy on the course and out in public. These remarks people make to me, the fact that they seek me out to tell me these things, tell me how well he was raised. Hearing that, I can think fondly of my father. His success in raising me has continued unbroken through our family. It is an honor to see it in action and to hear that people still appreciate those values he taught us. And I look forward to my great-grandchildren being raised in that same rich experience. That is the definition of a fabulous life.

CC and Margie Sabathia | Just Have Fun

CC Sabathia is a pitcher with the New York Yankees, and he helped win the 2009 World Series. He won the AL Cy Young Award in 2007 with the Cleveland Indians. He is a perennial All-Star and the father of four.

Margie Sabathia is CC Sabathia's mother.

CC Sabathia: When I was a freshman, I played my first high school basketball game. I was on junior varsity, and going into the game, I was a little nervous. My mother was in the stands when a couple of guys scored over me and out-rebounded me. I will never forget facing my mom after that game.

When I got off the court, she talked to me about the game. She reminded me that I was the biggest and strongest kid out there. In fact, she told me I was playing soft. I was passive at that point, relying on my physical gifts to succeed in sports more than any heart of aggression. My mom said that I better foul out the next game or maybe she wouldn't want to be in the stands.

CC and Margie Sabathia

I will never forget that moment. It definitely changed my basketball season. The next game I went out there and threw myself around. I played aggressively, just like my mom suggested. She obviously kept coming to my games. In fact, between her and my dad, someone was at pretty much every game I ever played. But that moment really represents what my parents meant to me.

One time a kid hit a home run off him, and he got upset. I told him that other kids can do well, too.

Margie Sabathia: CC was always competitive. He wanted to play the infield or pitch. One time a kid hit a home run off him, and he got upset. I told him that other kids can do well, too. It is supposed to be fun at that age. You're a good ballplayer, dude. Enjoy your life.

CS: There is no doubt that I got my toughness, my bull-dog attitude, from my mom. It probably was not just from that one conversation after the basketball game, but that one stands out. It crossed over to baseball after that, too. I could always hit, catch, and throw strikes, but after that I pitched with emotion. When I got to the big leagues, I didn't know how to control it. In those early games, I would get mad at umpires or throw my glove.

Now I control that emotion. It is interesting because emotion and aggressiveness can be a double-edged sword. It can be great sometimes, but it can be bad if it is not going well. Sports, like life, are complicated like that.

Growing up, my dad taught me a lot of the skills I needed to excel at baseball. He didn't play sports, but he listened to everything and coached Little League. When I was young he would videotape me and have me watch it after the game. He'd point out where my swing was wrong. I rebelled against that, as any kid would, but it helped. He also would practice with me all the time. I remember times when he was supposed to take me to school but we would go to the batting cages instead. We'd get breakfast

I remember times when my dad was supposed to take me to school but we would go to the batting cages instead.... I know that might sound bad, skipping school, but you can't imagine how great that memory is for me now.

together, and then he'd hit me some grounders. I know that might sound bad, skipping school, but you can't imagine how great that memory is for me now.

My dad really showed me the mechanics of the game, but both my parents were there all the time for me. Even when I was young, they would do whatever I wanted to do. They made sure that they did whatever they could to help me succeed. I was an only child, but even considering that, I cannot remember a single time when I asked them to play with me that they said no.

My mom likes to tell me how I was an active kid from the beginning. I ran around the house all the time, pretending I was playing sports. We played board games and Ping-Pong together. At first she used to beat me, but she hasn't in a while. Growing up, my mom was almost like a sister to me. We were so close, and we talked about everything. That relationship carried through my entire life and has now crossed over to my kids.

MS: I called CC "the baby teddy bear." He was so much fun and never any problem. He always listened to me, but he had so much energy. He would run up and down the hall, pretending to run the bases. If I could have guaranteed I'd have another son like him, I would have had more kids.

CS: I can remember my mom getting into full gear and catching for me in the backyard. Unfortunately, she didn't have a catcher's mitt, only a normal glove. When I was 11,

I threw a pitch that hit her in the palm of the glove. That was the last time she was able to catch for me.

MS: CC was so busy. When he didn't have a game, he liked me to get into all the catching equipment and get the home plate out. I would squat down and be his catcher. I did that until he was 11, then I was done. One day the ball came at me so fast that I was like, what the heck! I told him, "Mommy can't catch you. I'm afraid."

Sabathia and "Little C"

CS: My mom helped me with sports, but I also saw that she was a good athlete. In the second grade, there was a parent/son competition at the school. My mom and I won best free throws and three-pointers. She played softball when I was a kid, too, so I learned from example. When I was young my parents always made sure that I had something to do, and it usually revolved around sports. I came from a very competitive family.

My mom helped me with sports, but I also saw that she was a good athlete. In the second grade, there was a parent/son competition at the school. My mom and I won best free throws and three-pointers.

After all of that, I can say that they are a huge reason why I became a successful athlete. I can say that the only reason I have gotten here is because of them. My mom made sure I was always doing the things I was supposed to do. They both gave me all of their support. I remember when I was already on my way and my dad, before he passed away, told me I was going to be an All-Star and win the Cy Young Award. At the time, I just wanted to do my thing and be a pitcher, but he told me I was better than that.

When I was drafted by the Cleveland Indians, my mother even helped negotiate my first contract. It was the end of June, and I was sitting around waiting for something to happen. I was at the house, in the small room, and I was practicing my pitching motion. My mom saw me and said that she needed to get me out of the house. She knew how restless I was. So she called Dan O'Dowd, and 15 minutes later I had a contract to sign. I signed it and was off and running. My agent was not so happy about that, but from her years supporting me, my mom knew exactly what I needed.

MS: You never stop being a parent. I still get nervous watching CC pitch. The first through the fourth innings, I am a wreck. I count the days between outings and see who he is scheduled to face next. The funny thing is that three days' rest doesn't bother him. He wants the ball.

CS: Now I am using the things my parents taught me in a whole new way. I am a father, and I find myself passing on some of the things that my parents taught me. I know I want my kids to stay humble and be respectful of everyone. My parents were big on that. I know sports will be part of life, but I just want my kids to have fun. When I play with them, I don't try to teach them anything. I just like it the way it is, and I try not to force anything on my son, Little C. At six, he is already a huge sports fanatic. He plays T-ball and basketball. He wants to play football when he turns seven. I'm just not sure if I am ready for that.

For me, sports were always fun. They were never forced on me. That's because I always I wanted to do it. Even when my dad was helping me, he'd say that since we were playing, he might as well work with me. With my son, it will be the same way. I don't want him to be burned out at 12. He won't play on travel teams. Instead, I want him to play the sports as they come, like I did.

MS: I am a sports person, and I enjoyed everything CC did. I do remember when he was in junior high and he had a problem with his grades. I made him sit out the basketball season. I told him that he could play anything he wanted, but he had to bring home the grades. He tested that, but only once.

CS: Sports have changed a lot. Not only are kids specializing in one sport at a young age, but they are specializing in one position. When I was a kid, I pitched, played left field, and played third base. I want it to be like that with my kids.

Luckily, I have a great partner in my wife, Amber. I have known her since she was 16 years old. She was always a great girl, but after Little C was born, her maternal instinct exploded. She works so hard she's like Super Mom now. She does whatever needs to be done. We're a great team.

I have also been blessed with great kids. Like I said, Little C is a sports nut. It is basketball season, so he always wants to be outside shooting hoops in his Kobe jersey and headband. Once baseball season starts, it will switch around. Once he got upset with his mom because she packed his pinstripe uniform for an away game instead of the gray one. He will sit down and watch an entire football or basketball game with me. It is great.

My daughter Jaden is different. She is a girl's girl. She loves My Little Pony and dolls. Right now, she has no interest in sports. It is refreshing. My younger daughter might have sports in her blood. She is still a toddler, but if you put a basketball in front of her, she goes crazy. I am excited about that.

MS: CC is a great father. He really takes the time to be with his kids. And Little C is just like him. And when he wants to play, CC plays, even if he is tired. They love to watch basketball and football together. That is what CC and I did when he was little.

CS: I am not saying it is easy to be a parent. Sometimes being a professional athlete makes it even harder. During the season I have to travel a lot, so I try to find time when I can be with the kids. Often that's driving them to school. Even better, sometimes they come to me. While I was at spring training, my son came down to spend a week with me. His mom and the other kids were back home. So it was a great time to bond with him. He watched me pitch in a grapefruit league game. Afterward we went to the back field and I hit him some grounders. He hit three buckets of balls. That night we went to a movie.

Those are the moments I live for. It is what is so special about being a parent, building the same kinds of memories I have from my childhood with my kids. If I could give parents any advice, it would be simple. Listen to your kids. Find out what they like. And like my parents did, make it fun. Who knows where the good times will lead.

Mark Preisler and Mark Schlereth | Conclusion

So why did we write this book? The answer is simple. Our children deserve better. They deserve the opportunities many of the contributors to this book received through the sacrifices their parents made. It's at the core of what makes America great.

The common theme throughout all these essays is time. As Lou Holtz says, "You spell love 't-i-m-e.'" There is no greater gift we can give to our children than our time. Every minute you can give them is sacred. All of the moments we share turn to memories, memories for our children to build on throughout their lives and pass along to their children when they become parents.

Life can get in the way. Sometimes everything seems more important. Just think, God forbid, if something happens. Put yourself in Jim Kelly's shoes. He knows just how important it is to appreciate every moment. None of us have any idea what the future might bring.

When you appreciate every moment, you instill the spirit to succeed in your children. Kirk Gibson's father did, and look what happened. Not only did Kirk hit one of the most memorable home runs in World Series lore, but he passed on that spirit to his children. In turn, they will pass it to their children. That spirit will live forever.

There will always be excuses. Maybe work is too demanding. Jim Craig's dad worked long hours seven days a week, and he was met in the driveway by his kids, gloves in hand. He could have gone inside, watched TV, had a beer, but he didn't. He played with his kids because it was a priority to him.

There will also be challenges to overcome. Think about what Amy Van Dyken's parents faced. Their daughter had life-threatening asthma, yet she led an active life as a child. If her parents could overcome their fear to do what was best for Amy, none of us have an excuse not to be active with our children.

Many people feel that society has changed. Kids don't have the freedom they once did. If that is true and we cannot allow our kids to play football in the street or walk to school on their own, it is up to us to do it with them. Don't use it as an excuse; use it as motivation. Let the dishes pile up, ignore your smart phone, and get down on the ground and get dirty playing with your kids.

From Laila Ali's story, you can see just how important spending time with your kids can be. Without building that relationship, you will never have the opportunity to change your child's path when it needs to be changed. As most of the contributors said, this is our one chance, and the years go by fast. If we don't start now, it may well be too late.

Maybe your kids won't want to push a truck like Mike Golic and his brothers did. They might not have a passion for sports. What is common among almost everyone who contributed to this work is finding out what your child is into and supporting them. Give them time, and spell it "l-o-v-e." It is the best investment you can make in life.

As George Foreman put it, children give us a purpose in life. So we urge you to take an active role in your kids' lives and in the lives of others. Pick a foundation mentioned in the Contributors' Charities section, make a donation, or volunteer your time. As George Foreman says, "It doesn't matter how many jobs you work, you are going to find time somewhere to relax or go play with your friends. Those hours you take for yourself you have to give to your kids. You've got to just do it."

Appendix | Contributors' Charities

Laila Ali

The Women's Sports Foundation was founded by Billie Jean King in 1974. It is the leading authority on the participation of women and girls in sports and advocates for equality, and it educates the public, conducts research, and offers grants to promote sports and physical activity for girls and women. The foundation's work shapes public attitude about women's sports and athletes, builds capacity for organizations that get girls active, provides equal opportunities for girls and women, and supports physically and emotionally healthy lifestyles. For more information, contact:

> Women's Sports Foundation
> 1899 Hempstead Turnpike, Suite 400
> East Meadow, NY 11554
> (800) 227-3988
> info@womenssportsfoundation.org
> www.womenssportsfoundation.org

Jim Craig

The Ultimate SAAAve is an organization dedicated to saving lives by educating the public on the dangers of Abdominal

Aortic Aneurysms. Jim Craig has championed the cause of AAA screening since his father passed away from the condition. He is dedicated to educating people around the country about this disease and how to defeat it. For more information, contact:

>ultimatesAAAve@wlgore.com
>www.ultimatesaaave.org

Herm Edwards

The Juvenile Diabetes Research Foundation International is a worldwide leader in funding research to cure Type 1 (juvenile) diabetes. They are also working with researchers to develop new treatments that can improve the lives of those suffering from the disease. For more information, contact:

>Juvenile Diabetes Research Foundation
>   International
>26 Broadway, 14th Floor
>New York, NY 10004
>(800) 533-CURE (2873)
>info@jdrf.org
>www.jdrf.org

Mike Eruzione

Winthrop Charities was founded after Mike Eruzione's mother passed away. He won $125,000 on *Who Wants To Be a Millionaire*, which helped put in a high school gym to support healthy active lifestyles for teenagers. It also helps pay user fees for disadvantaged kids to take part in recreational and school sports. For more information, contact:

>Winthrop Charities
>28 Thornton Street
>Winthrop, MA 02152

George Foreman

George Foreman built the George Foreman Youth & Community Center in 1984 with money he saved through his eight-year retirement. He wanted to create a haven for kids to hang out. One of the reasons Foreman reentered boxing was to continue to support the center.

> The George Foreman Youth & Community Center
> 2202 Lone Oak
> Houston, TX 77093
> (218) 987-8743
> www.biggeorge.com

Julie Foudy

The Julie Foudy Leadership Foundation is a nonprofit public-funded charity founded on the belief that within every girl and young woman there is a leader. In an effort to inspire today's young women to become tomorrow's leaders, the foundation embraces the concept that sports provide an ideal training vehicle. Participating in sports often allows young women to discover their inner strength, their voice, and ultimately their ability to positively impact society. For more information, contact:

> The Julie Foudy Leadership Foundation
> 806 E. Avenida Pico, Suite I, #318
> San Clemente, CA 92673
> (949) 648-2050
> www.foudyleadershipfoundation.org

Steve Garvey

A California native, Garvey is proud to support Youth Baseball of Palm Desert, which provides Little League baseball for children in the Palm Desert region of eastern California. For more information, or to make a donation, please write:

Youth Baseball of Palm Desert
74-923 Highway 11
Indian Wells, CA 92210

Grant Hill

The Tamia and Grant Hill Foundation is located in Orlando, Florida. Through their foundation they have donated time and money to charities, schools, scholarships, nonprofit organizations, and churches. Most of their donations support children's and educational charities. For more information, visit:

www.granthill.com/giving-back/national.php

Lou Holtz

The Lou Holtz Charitable Foundation was founded in 1998 by Lou Holtz and his wife Beth. Its mission is to promote Christianity, education, and charity through fund-raising activities as well as private and corporate donations. The foundation donates to nonprofits such as Touching Tiny Lives that support its mission. TTL provides food, medical care, and outreach to children in great need of stabilization and services. For more information on TTL, contact:

Touching Tiny Lives Foundation USA
11415 Manor Road
Leawood, KS 66211
info@touchingtinylives.org
www.touchingtinylives.org

Jim Kelly

Hunter's Hope was established in memory of Jim Kelly's son to address the acute need for information and research with respect to Krabbe disease and related leukodystrophies. In addition, they strive to support and encourage those afflicted and their families as they struggle to endure, adjust, and cope with the demands of these fatal illnesses. Among the essential goals, founders Jim and Jill Kelly seek to inspire an appreciation of all children and express a thankful heart toward God for these precious gifts of life. These bedrock values are categorically and vigilantly expressed throughout all of the foundation's programs and activities. For more information, contact:

> Hunter's Hope Foundation
> P.O. Box 643
> 6368 West Quaker Street
> Orchard Park, NY 14127
> (716) 667-1200
> info@huntershope.org
> www.huntershope.org

Arnold Palmer

The Arnold Palmer Medical Center Foundation was established in the 1980s to help build a hospital in Orlando, Florida, that would provide comprehensive medical care for children and women, leading to the Arnold Palmer Hospital for Children and Women. It has since grown into a full medical center, with the addition of the Winnie Palmer Hospital for Women and Babies. The Arnold Palmer Medical Foundation serves as the community outreach arm of the medical center, seeking philanthropic funding from individuals, private and corporate foundations, and community and civic organizations. For more information, contact:

> Arnold Palmer Medical Center Foundation
> 3160 Southgate Commerce Blvd., Suite 50
> Orlando, FL 32806
> (407) 841-5114

Cal Ripken Jr.

The Cal Ripken Sr. Foundation is a nonprofit organization working throughout the country with Boys and Girls Clubs, PAL Centers, inner-city schools, and other organizations serving America's most distressed communities. The foundation helps to build character and teach critical life lessons to disadvantaged young people through baseball- and softball-themed programs. For more information, contact:

> Cal Ripken Sr. Foundation
> 1427 Clarkview Road, Suite 100
> Baltimore, MD 21209
> (877) RIPKEN1
> info@ripkenfoundation.org
> www.ripkenfoundation.org

Nolan Ryan

The Nolan Ryan Foundation was founded in 1990 by Nolan and Ruth Ryan, who generously give their time for fundraising efforts that provide the foundation resources for youth, education, and community development. For more information, contact:

> Nolan Ryan Foundation
> 2925 South Bypass 35
> Alvin, TX 77511
> (281) 388-1134
> www.nolanryanfoundation.org

CC Sabathia

The PitCCh In Foundation is dedicated to enriching the lives of inner-city youth by working to raise self-esteem through education and athletic activities. They partner with such organizations as Toys for Tots and the Boys and Girls Clubs. For more information, contact:

www.pitcchinfoundation.org
info@pitcchinfoundation.org

Amy Van Dyken

The Leukemia and Lymphoma Society is the world's largest voluntary health organization dedicated to funding blood cancer research, education, and patient services. Their mission is to cure leukemia, lymphoma, Hodgkin's disease, and myeloma, and to improve the quality of life of patients and their families. Amy Van Dyken's father is a recent survivor. For more information, contact:

The Leukemia and Lymphoma Society
1311 Mamaroneck Avenue, Suite 310
White Plains, NY 10605
(888) 773-9958
www.lls.org

Photo Credits